Needlepoint

By the Editors of Sunset Books and Sunset Magazine

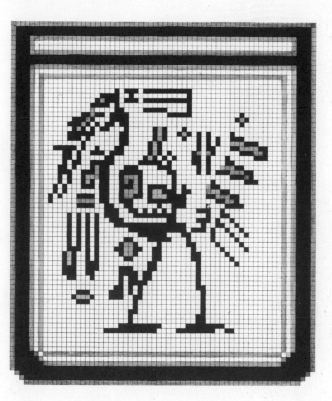

LANE BOOKS · MENLO PARK, CALIFORNIA

Foreword

With yarn, canvas, needle, and a bit of confidence, the world of needlepointing is open to you. No longer do you have to rely solely on the professionally designed needlepoint canvases; you can design your own, transfer the pattern to your canvas, stitch it, then block and finish the needlepoint project completely by yourself. This book offers the basic needlepoint techniques, as well as projects that range from petit point brooches to a wastebasket cover. The possibilities are endless, so come join the thousands of other women, men, and children who have discovered the pleasures of needlepoint.

Contributing to the many innovative designs and techniques in this book, we acknowledge with gratitude Mrs. Phalice Ayers, Mrs. Lillian Jane Feight Del Carlo, Mrs. Bard K. Dowse, and Mrs. Nelson Nowell. Our thanks also go to John Flack, Lawrence A. Laukhuf, and Joe Seney for their consultation on the book design.

Edited by Susan Sedlacek Lampton

Photographs and Drawings by Alyson Smith Gonsalves
Project Pattern Charts by Annette Gilson Carlson
Cover: The start of a needlepoint pillow (pages 36-47).
Floral design by Alyson S. Gonsalves.
Photographed by George Selland, Moss Photography.
Cover design: John Flack.

Executive Editor, Sunset Books: David E. Clark

Contents

SECTION I

An Introduction to Needlepoint

SECTION II

Needlepoint Projects for Everyone

SPECIAL FEATURES

An Introduction to Needlepoint

**History • Equipment • Basic stitches
Decorative stitches • Techniques**

Needlepoint: The Renaissance of a Gracious Craft

With painting (which it so closely resembles), needlepoint has at least two qualities in common: 1) it is done on a canvas, and 2) its nature has changed dramatically over recent years.

Needlepoint has shifted from its earlier emphasis on formal, somber floral patterns into a whole new imaginative era. What has caused the dramatic renaissance of this craft has been the emergence of boldly imaginative designs — often original; of bright new yarn colors; and, most of all, of needlepoint craftsmen, both women and men, who are willing to expand beyond time-honored patterns and techniques. In our craft-conscious age, the vigor and popularity of needlepoint are at a new peak.

Needlepoint offers a creative outlet with many advantages. It can be a hobby requiring merely a relaxed hand movement as you fill in a canvas's background area while chatting with a friend or even watching television. Or it can be infinitely more demanding — a skill requiring your utmost absorption as you stitch around a fine, complex design. Needlepoint is an eminently portable craft: you can roll up your canvas, needle, and yarn into a small parcel, digging into it to pass the hours on your commuter train, vacation drive, or trans-Pacific flight. Perhaps neatness is all-important to you? If so, needlepoint is the perfect craft: no spilled paint, no scraps of cut material, no sticky glue. And for the person who values his uniqueness, an original, handstitched piece of needlework is a handsome rebuttal to anybody's computer. The ultimate pleasure of needlepoint is that it allows you to express your creativity and originality.

For men, needlepoint offers the same advantages and pleasures that it does for women. Although some men feel they are not particularly adept with a needle, it is surprising how far you can go in needlework with a minimum of basic training or skill. The size of your stitch is determined by the gauge of canvas you're using, and wool yarns come in a variety of colors ranging from the most soft-spoken to the most vocal. The needle is so blunt that it is almost impossible to prick your finger. Certainly one does not need even to be able to sew on a button to become a successful needlepointer. Perhaps the greatest challenge is attaining a smoothly stitched surface, but anyone can learn the fundamentals of needlepoint in an hour.

Needlepoint yesterday. The date of origin of needlepoint — as of all needlework — can never be firmly fixed. But we do know that decorative stitching was used to embellish garments of ancient Egyptians.

COURTESY, MUSEUM OF FINE ARTS, BOSTON

16th CENTURY EUROPEAN needlework illustrates concern for detail and fine tedious stitching.

Needlepoint as we know it — embroidery stitches worked on an open-weave canvas — became popular in the 16th century. Probably the greatest stimulus of this craft was the introduction of the steel needle in Elizabethan England as well as pattern books that were published later. Soon needlepoint was found in nearly every European household. The hours that Princess Elizabeth passed in the Tower of London were made more bearable by the needlepoint stitching she did there.

Needlepoint crossed the Atlantic to take hold in colonial America. Here it was used in samplers, as upholstery fabric, and for fashion accessories. Although most designs showed a strong European influence, Americans soon developed their own patterns. Because of the cost of importing yarns, colonial women spun their yarn then dyed it with leaves and berries.

Early needlepoint was done on a loosely woven linen material. Eventually, single-thread canvases were made especially for this craft. After double-mesh canvas was

COMPARISON of early colonial needlework with present day pieces accentuates the great style changes that all handcrafts experience. A definite trend toward abstract design and simple patterns makes today's needlepoint so distinguishable.

invented by a Frenchman in the 1860's, needlepoint burgeoned as a popular craft. The double-thread canvas was often worked in a combination of fine petit point stitches suitable for fine detail and larger (gros point) stitches. To allow this combination, double meshes were separated to form a single-thread area for petit point work.

Although interest in needlepoint faded at the beginning of the 20th century, it has enjoyed nothing less than an overwhelming popularity in the past few years. Today, needlepoint has become one of the favorite means of expression for the creative needleworker — the craftsman whose piece of contemporary beauty can become, in time, not only a family heirloom but also a collector's item.

Needlepoint today. Needlepoint seems especially suited to an age in which the word "tension" is on everyone's lips. The Oriental philosopher well summed up the craft's delights when he wrote, "One joy dispels a hundred cares." Most needleworkers will agree that their stitching provides an ideal respite from the surge of every day living.

Traditionally, needlepoint has been used to create wall hangings, fine pictures, throw pillows, and pincushions. But today the scope of the craft has broadened to include belts, wastebaskets, clock faces, handbags, vests, pockets, and eyeglass cases.

When you begin a needlepoint project, you'll be in the distinguished company of many celebrities. Even Picasso contributed to the craft: he designed stunning abstract canvases as backs and seats for two chairs that were stitched for Gertrude Stein by Alice B. Toklas.

If you don't have a Picasso to fall back on, patterns to fit every personality are available on pre-painted canvases. Or the excitement of designing, stitching, and finishing your own pattern awaits you in this instructional text. Whether you are a beginner or an expert, this book is designed to inspire and guide you into entering the special world of needlepoint.

Needlepoint Materials and Equipment

Needlepoint can be a relatively inexpensive medium, particularly if you do all the designing, stitching, and finishing yourself. The modest needs for material and equipment probably help to account for the increasing popularity of this handcraft. From the following lists, you can choose those few items necessary for personal success in needlepoint.

CANVAS, THE BASIC MATERIAL

Although the word "canvas" may suggest heavy material used for boat sails or the dense cloth on which a painter makes his brush strokes, canvas is not always closely woven. Needlepoint canvas, for example, resembles coarse window screening. Usually made from heavily-starched cotton, it is available in either white or ecru and a light yellow in the finer mesh canvases. White cotton, the most commonly used canvas, is more popular than ecru because the needlepoint designer often chooses to paint a design directly onto the canvas with acrylic paints before starting to needlepoint (see page 39). The paint pigment is more visible on the white cotton than on the dark ecru. Ecru canvas, some feel, has the advantage of being much stronger than the white. A detailed discussion of the types of canvases and other necessary information follows.

What types of canvases are available? Choice of canvas is a major factor in your needlepoint design. Canvas comes in many gauges (threads per inch) and in two different mesh formations. (Mesh refers to the intersection of horizontal and vertical threads in the weave of the canvas.) In mono (or single mesh) canvas, the weave consists of single horizontal threads woven an even distance from single vertical threads. Penelope canvas, on the other hand, is double threaded, each mesh of the weave consisting of an intersection of two slightly spaced horizontal threads and two very close vertical threads.

Most stitches can be executed on either mono or Penelope canvas. The greatest difference between the two types is that Penelope — the more versatile — allows you to take both petit point and gros point stitches on the same canvas. At first you might find it much easier to work on mono canvas because of its single-thread mesh. But try both types of canvas, and then decide for yourself which you should use for a particular project.

Choosing the correct gauge of canvas. Gauge of the canvas tells how many threads, either single or double

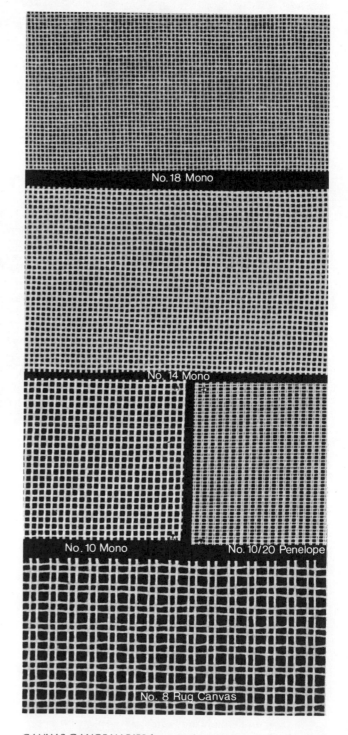

CANVAS GAUGE VARIES from petit point canvas for detailed designs to rug-sized canvas for bolder patterns.

mesh, the canvas has to the inch. For example, a number 10 mono canvas has ten threads to the inch, so a design executed on number 10 canvas will have ten stitches per inch (see example below, left).

The same size in double mesh or Penelope will be indicated by the figure 10/20. As on mono canvas, ten gros point stitches can be executed in 1 inch, or the paired vertical threads can be spread apart to create petit point stitches for a total of 20 stitches in 1 inch (see example below, right).

Gauges of canvas vary from an extremely fine mesh to the considerably larger rug canvas. A few canvas swatches shown at left illustrate the wide range of sizes. When working on a canvas with 16 threads per inch or more, you are stitching in petit point. Work done on canvas 14 threads per inch or less is considered gros point.

Canvases come in different widths, normally ranging from 24 to 36 or 40 inches. Some canvases, such as rug canvas, are even wider. The finer the canvas (the more threads to the square inch), the narrower the width. Most finer mesh canvases will be 24 inches wide.

Purchasing good canvas. Shopping for canvas will make the greatest demands on your wallet. On an average, you will pay about $6.00 to $8.00 a yard (depending on the mesh and type of canvas) — but a yard of canvas will keep you in stitches for weeks!

The canvas you purchase should be free of any flaws. Watch for such defects as knotted, joined, thin, or weak threads in the weave. When the needlepoint is drying during the blocking, a great strain occurs that could cause these weak points to snap and ruin your piece. In buying canvas, look for stock with a sheen or glossy appearance. This indicates that the canvas has been coated with a sizing that will keep it from becoming limp and misshapen as you stitch. Make sure that it has evenly woven squares.

Penelope or mono canvas? By reading the descriptions above, you may have already decided on the type of canvas you will use. If not, some further considerations may be helpful.

Mono canvas is easy on your eyes while you work. Because you stitch over an intersection of only two threads on mono canvas as compared with four on Penelope canvas, you will be less confused about which square your stitch should be taken in.

On the other hand, although some feel Penelope canvas is more difficult to work with, you will be able to create curved shapes and details more easily on it than on mono because you can take petit point stitches where necessary. In addition some consider Penelope canvas stronger because it has four canvas threads interwoven and "locked" into position at each intersection, whereas mono canvas has only two threads at each intersection.

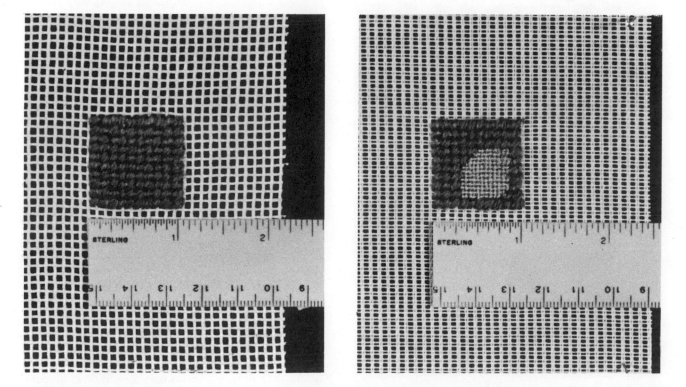

MONO CANVAS, with 10 threads to the inch, will carry 10 stitches per inch. PENELOPE CANVAS, with 10 double threads to the inch will carry 10 regular stitches but 20 petit point stitches when canvas threads are separated.

A variation of the mono canvas (shown below) has been developed which is a compromise between both mono and Penelope. It has double threads, like the Penelope, making it as strong but not as versatile because the doubled threads can't be separated for petit point work. Its greatest advantage is that the tightly woven double threads don't slip as you stitch, a characteristic of most mono canvases.

Canvases for special purposes. Several specialized canvases are available that meet certain needlepoint needs. A canvas made just for Bargello stitching (see page 32) holds its shape better than the regular canvas and, because of small fibers along the canvas threads, prevents vertical stitches from separating. Another unusual canvas has flat threads instead of the normal round ones for ease in mitering corners.

Other special canvases include plastic or perforated paper. Paper canvas resembles the little sampler cards you may have stitched as a child. Even though the disadvantages of these two canvases are obvious, children might find them easier to handle. Most children, however, will prefer working on number 10 cotton mono canvas or the larger rug-sized canvases.

Specialty canvases are not always carried by needlework stores, but nearly anything which is evenly woven can be used as a ground for needlepoint. You might even experiment with embroidery cloth.

DOUBLE WEAVE MONO CANVAS is stronger than regular mono canvas. Plastic canvas (bottom) appeals to children.

NEEDLEPOINT YARNS: "PIGMENT" FOR YOUR CANVAS

Yarn shops today display a rich variety of types, an explosion of colors. Though shoppers may be dazzled by the kaleidoscopic offering of yarns, they will want to consider carefully not only color but also quality.

One characteristic of needlepoint yarn is more important than any other. Fibers of the yarn must be long and somewhat smooth so that, after extensive tugging and pulling through the holes of the canvas, the yarn will not fluff up or wear thin. Knitting worsted yarns are not as satisfactory as yarns made specifically for canvas work because the fibers are short and will fluff up as well as break easily. Although worsted yarns are not as strong as some of the needlepoint yarns, worsted can be used for any items you do not expect to keep as heirlooms. Because most yarns today are mothproof as well as colorfast, they are extremely durable.

What types of yarns are available? Some consider Persian wools the best for needlepoint because they are versatile and come in a multitude of colors. Persian yarns come in strands of three threads loosely twisted together. The advantage of this yarn is that it can be used as one large thread for gros point work or separated for petit point work. Persian wool can be purchased by weight or, in some instances, by the single strand.

Some disadvantages of Persian wools: they are not always available, they are one of the most expensive yarns, and the single threads can get pulled out of place giving an uneven look to your stitching.

Tapestry wool is a four-ply yarn (four tightly twisted strands) that can also be separated into single strands, but not as easily as the Persian wool. Some people prefer to work with tapestry yarn because it is considerably less expensive, and comes in a variety of skein sizes. Though the color selection for tapestry is not as extensive as for Persian wool, its availability makes it a popular yarn.

Although much finer than the Persian or tapestry yarns, crewel embroidery wool yarn can also be used for canvas work. One strand of crewel yarn is comparable in size to just one strand of the Persian yarn, making it ideal for petit point work. At the other end of the spectrum of yarn sizes, rug wool is most often used for rug-sized canvases, but some of the rug wools can be used on 10 or even 12 mesh canvas.

In addition to wools, many cotton, silk, and synthetic yarns are adaptable to needlepoint. Fine-quality pearl cotton has a distinguishing luster that other cotton yarns do not have. When any cotton yarn is used, individual stitches acquire a distinctive appearance, so it is important that you choose a weight that will cover the canvas completely. (A number 3 pearl cotton is a good weight for canvas work.)

Cotton yarns can be found in both two-ply and six-ply sizes. Commonly called embroidery floss, six-ply yarn has one disadvantage; its individual strands can easily become looped or pulled out of place as you stitch. This is why most needleworkers prefer the pearl cotton.

Embroidery silk also comes in six-ply strands. Since silk is very expensive, it works best for small areas or highlights in a piece. Rayon is also best used in small areas or highlights. It has an even greater sheen than silk but costs much less. Both silk and rayon have a slippery quality, making them difficult to work with.

Experiment with many yarns, and familiarize yourself with the selection your local needlework stores offer. Here is a way to keep a record of your discoveries: stitch some small squares of canvas with different yarn samples; then label them according to cost, colors available, size of skeins, and how much yarn it took to stitch a given area. Keep this information in a file as a constant source.

What type of yarn for which canvas? The guide shown on page 12 tells in general terms the weight of yarn, number of strands, and size of needle used on the different gauge canvases. Because everyone has a different "tension" in their stitching, stitches on some canvases may require more yarn strands than those suggested in the chart.

DETERMINING HOW MUCH YARN TO BUY

If you want to avoid the process of measuring, sampling, and multiplying to discover the amount of yarn required for a project, most needlework shop clerks will be glad to look at your design and estimate the amount of yarn needed. After completing several pieces, you will be able to predict your own yarn purchases fairly accurately.

1. Select the type and size of yarn you will use for your needlepoint project, keeping in mind the mesh and size of the canvas.
2. Cut some measured lengths of the same type of yarn, and work a one-inch square in the stitch you plan to use.
3. Approximate the number of square inches in your canvas design to be covered in each color.
4. Multiply the number of square inches on the canvas in each color by the length of yarn used in the 1-inch square.
5. The total of this calculation should give the approximate amount of yarn to purchase in each color. Add several inches to each total for good measure.

MOST POPULAR YARNS are shown above, but don't hesitate to experiment with ribbon, raffia or other unusual threads. The only requirement is that the yarn cover the canvas sufficiently and withstand constant pulling as you stitch.

COORDINATING CANVAS, YARN, AND NEEDLE SIZES

Use this chart as a general guide for selecting yarn, canvas, and needle sizes. Everyone stitches differently, so sizes should be determined strictly by what is comfortable for you.

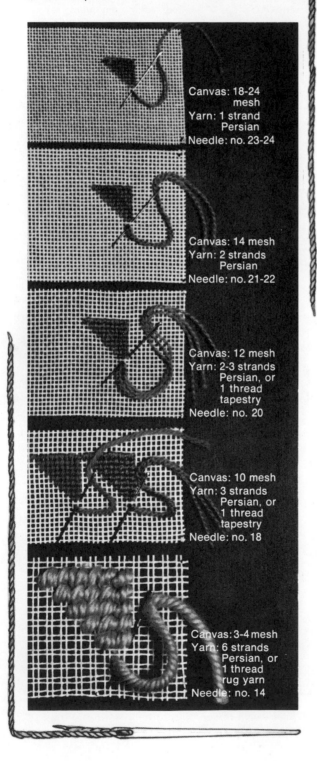

Canvas: 18-24 mesh
Yarn: 1 strand Persian
Needle: no. 23-24

Canvas: 14 mesh
Yarn: 2 strands Persian
Needle: no. 21-22

Canvas: 12 mesh
Yarn: 2-3 strands Persian, or 1 thread tapestry
Needle: no. 20

Canvas: 10 mesh
Yarn: 3 strands Persian, or 1 thread tapestry
Needle: no. 18

Canvas: 3-4 mesh
Yarn: 6 strands Persian, or 1 thread rug yarn
Needle: no. 14

Follow these two general rules in determining the weight of yarn to select: (1) if you have difficulty pulling the yarn through the mesh, or if the stitches do not fit easily but have a tendency to hump, you are using a thicker strand than is necessary; (2) if the canvas shows through the stitches, you are not using a sufficiently thick thread.

How much yarn should you buy? Yarn is usually sold by weight or in pre-measured skeins, but needlework stores will sometimes sell single strands or very small amounts (particularly in Persian wools).

The safest rule to follow when purchasing yarn for a project is to buy more than enough because extra yarn will always be of some use later. Nothing is more distressing than to run out of yarn before finishing a project. If you try to purchase more, you might find that the dye lot of the yarn has changed just enough to make the new shade incompatible with the original color in your design.

To be as accurate as possible in determining amounts, use the formula shown on page 11 to estimate the quantities needed. (Normally, one 40 yard skein will cover an area 9 x 3 inches on number 12 canvas.) Take into consideration differences in the amount of yarn used in different stitches. The basketweave stitch (page 18) will require a little more yarn than the continental stitch (page 16), and all the additional decorative stitches (pages 22-35) will vary according to the size of the canvas and the stitch used.

NEEDLES FOR NEEDLEPOINT

Needlepoint needles (also called tapestry needles) come in varying sizes, corresponding to the gauge of your canvas and to the thickness of your yarn. In choosing the correct needle, consider these two essential points: (1) the needle, when pulled through the canvas hole should not distort it; (2) the eye of the needle should be large enough to carry the required size of yarn.

Needles vary in size from number 24, one of the smallest, to number 14, one of the largest (see photograph at right). All needles have a blunt point so that they will not split the threads of the canvas and a large eye for easy threading. For help in determining which needle to work with, refer to the chart on the left.

Sizes 21-24 are considered petit point needles. Sizes 18, 19, and 20 are commonly considered gros point needles. Size 18 is a popular needle, the one you probably will use for most of your gros point needlepoint projects.

Tapestry needles can be purchased singly, in packages of one size, or in packages with several different sizes. You may want to keep a variety of sizes on hand, storing them in a protective container. Another worthwhile purchase is an inexpensive pincushion with an attached "strawberry emery." If your needle should begin to "drag" while you stitch, poke the point into the emery. This cleans off the needle and makes it travel easier between the canvas meshes. Needles and pincushions can be purchased in most five and dime stores or in any needlecraft store.

MISCELLANEOUS EQUIPMENT

Like the automobile buyer, the worker in needlepoint finds that his initial investment can be enhanced by the purchase of several accessories. But unlike the automobile buyer, the needlepoint craftsman will not have to do violence to his bank account in order to afford these helpful extras.

The following list suggests accessories — some necessary, some pleasantly useful — for your needlework:

1. A pair of small scissors is a necessity. Choose a good brand with sharp pointed blades. These are useful for snipping yarn ends and, hopefully not too often, for cutting out mistakes.

2. A thimble is not essential, but it does protect fingers from becoming tender, especially if you work at needlepoint for several hours at a time. If the thimble seems more a burden than useful, try wrapping your finger with a band-aid so that the pad protects the portion of your finger you use to push the needle through the canvas.

3. An indelible marking pen can be used to draw the outline of your design onto the canvas (see page 39). Be certain the pen is absolutely indelible so that it will not run when you wet your piece for blocking. First test the pen on a small piece of canvas, and then submerge the sample in water. If you plan to spray your needlepoint with a protective coating to make it waterproof or stain-resistant, test the pen by spraying an inked swatch of canvas to see that the ink does not run.

4. Acrylic paints are also used for transferring a design to canvas. They are indelible, easy to work with, and come in a wide variety of colors. To provide yourself with an accurate color guide as you stitch, paint the entire design in the same colors as those of the yarn you plan to use (see page 39).

5. Graph paper is for the needlepointer who wants an accurate guide to work from but does not want to trace the design directly onto the canvas (see page 40). Graph paper can be purchased in tablets or single large sheets from most stationery stores. Tracing paper is handy to have for copying design ideas from magazines or photographs.

6. Stationary frames for holding canvas are available in some needlecraft stores. However, these are rarely used for anything smaller than a rug-sized canvas.

An aid to needlepointers who are often bothered by all the extra canvas, plastic rods are available that have a slot in which you attach the needlepoint canvas edge. The needlepoint can be rolled to expose just the area being worked.

7. Masking tape or a plastic-coated cloth tape can be used to bind off the edges of canvas. Covering the edges with tape prevents raveling and keeps yarn from catching as you stitch. (Use 1-inch tape.)

8. Rust-proof T-pins or aluminum tacks will be necessary if you plan to block your projects. A firm but soft board should be used as the support during the blocking process. Use an artist's drawing board or a piece of soft pine purchased from the lumber yard.

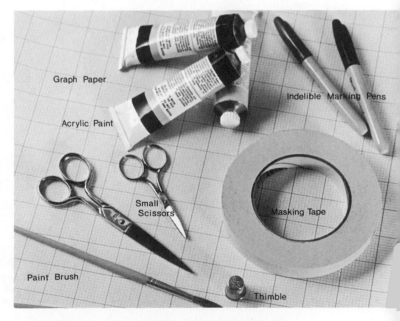

NEEDLE SIZES VARY with the canvas and yarn used. Extra equipment is not necessary but sometimes helpful.

Learning the Basic Needlepoint Stitch

Traditionally, the craft of needlepoint has long been based on one simple basic stitch. Today, however, the approach to needlepoint has broadened. In addition to the original basic stitch, many other decorative stitches have been added, stitches that are worked either diagonally or vertically across the meshes and that cover more than a single mesh.

Although these decorative stitches are really a form of "canvas embroidery," needlepointers are beginning to use them more frequently to add texture or interest to their designs. A few of these stitches are discussed on pages 22-35.

Because the first section of this book has been written for the beginning needlepoint enthusiast, it emphasizes mastering the technique of the basic stitch. This stitch always covers one intersection of a horizontal and vertical canvas thread and slants from lower left to upper right. The basic needlepoint stitch can be achieved by using one of two stitching techniques, the continental (tent stitch) or the basketweave (bias tent stitch).

Both of these techniques will provide you with a means for limitless needlepoint designing on either mono or Penelope canvas. Although the two methods produce what appears to be the same slanting stitch,

each is achieved in an entirely different manner. You should be aware of the advantages and disadvantages of both techniques.

The continental is easy to learn and can be stitched horizontally and diagonally right to left or vertically top to bottom (if you are right-handed). It works well for single lines, color accents, and small areas.

If you use the continental stitch extensively in a piece, however, you will find upon completion that your image is pulled noticeably in one direction. This is not irreparable, but you may need to block it several times to return the piece to its original horizontal and vertical lines. The second major disadvantage of the continental is that once a row is completed, you must turn the entire canvas around to begin the second row, because you always work from right to left (if you are right-handed).

Somewhat more difficult to learn, the basketweave may very well become your favorite stitch. Basketweave is most often used in large undecorated areas, rather than in small, intricately-designed ones, because the order of stitching becomes quite confusing in a small area with many different colors or patterns.

One advantage of basketweave is that the rows are worked on a diagonal, so you do not need to turn the

IDENTICAL FROM THE TOP VIEW, the two techniques used in producing the basic stitch are identifiable by the pattern created on the backside. Continental (middle) has slanting stitches; basketweave (right) has interwoven threads.

canvas as you stitch each row. Another advantage is that a thick interwoven pattern is produced on the underside of the canvas (see comparison of backs of continental and basketweave opposite page). Very little distortion is evident in the completed piece because of the uniformity of the interwoven threads on the underside. This makes blocking of a predominantly basket-woven piece considerably easier than blocking one done entirely in the continental stitch.

Continental and basketweave stitches can be used together or interchanged as often as required in a single piece. The main concern is that the stitches are all slanting in the same direction (normally, lower left to upper right). Learn both basic techniques so that, when you begin a project, you can concentrate on the pattern or design you are creating rather than on the mechanics of the stitching.

In the following instructions and photographs, two steps are always combined into one continuous move-ment to eliminate both wasted time and confusion. Each individual stitch could be worked by moving from the face of the canvas to the underside and back again. But by using the single motion, you don't need to work on the underside of the canvas until you tie off an end or begin a new thread. In most instances, the com-pletion of one stitch and the start of the next stitch is always the single step as shown in the photographs.

The terms "mesh" and "row" are used throughout the stitch directions. Mesh always refers to the vertical threads or the intersection of a vertical and horizontal thread. Row always refers to a row of spaces or holes. As an example: one mesh to the left and two rows below the corner of a square drawn on the canvas would look like the illustration below. The needle would be pulled to the face of the canvas through the hole with the dot.

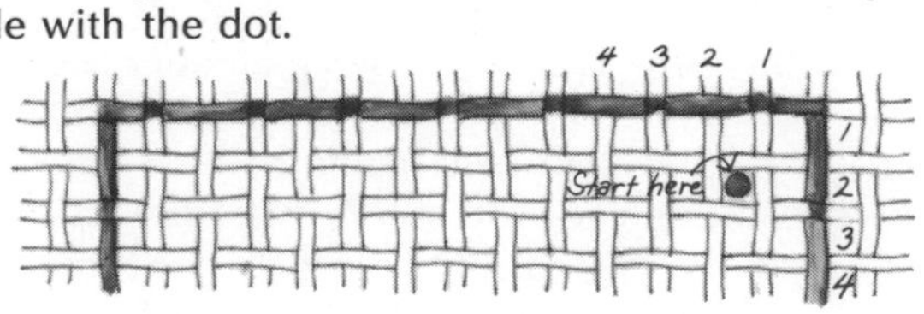

![Illustration of canvas mesh with numbers 4 3 2 1 across top and 1 2 3 4 down right side, "Start here" label with dot]

Notice that mono (or single mesh) canvas was used in the demonstration photographs. If you prefer to practice on the Penelope (or double mesh) canvas, make sure that each stitch covers two paired horizontal canvas threads and two paired vertical threads.

How to thread your needle and begin a length of yarn are explained in the box on the right. Use these methods as you practice the basic and decorative stitches.

Note to the left-handed stitcher: all instructions have been written for the right-handed needleworker. In some instances you will have to reverse the instruc-tions and think of the photographs upside down. Be-fore each set of instructions for the basic and decora-tive stitches, brief directions are given if the left-hand-ed person should do anything different from what follows.

STARTING AND ENDING A THREAD

THREADING A NEEDLE

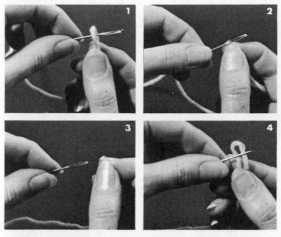

Loop yarn over needle. Grasp yarn between thumb and finger, pull tightly against needle. Remove nee-dle. Force needle eye down on yarn and pull through.

STARTING A LENGTH OF YARN (TWO METHODS)

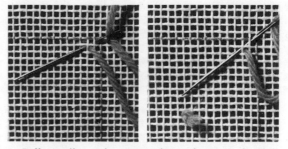

1. Pull needle and yarn to face of canvas leaving 1-inch tail on underside. Weave tail into back of first stitches or 2. Knot yarn tail, pull needle from face to underside of canvas below starting point. Begin stitch-ing at starting point. Cut off knot after stitching several rows.

ENDING A LENGTH OF YARN

Weave end of yarn into back of stitches, against then back towards direction of stitching or at right angles to the row. To start next length, start as above or weave end of yarn into back of stitches.

DETAIL OF SAMPLER, page 22, shows that single lines and small areas are best when done in the continental.

THE CONTINENTAL STITCH

To begin, bind the edges of a small piece of canvas approximately 6 inches by 6 inches. Then, using an indelible marker, draw a 2-inch square on the canvas (an inch away from the top and side edge).

Note to left-handed workers: turn the photographs upside down and reverse instructions. Work from left to right, bottom to top.

Cut a length of yarn approximately 30 inches long, and thread it onto a needle (see box, page 15). Draw the threaded needle from the underside of the canvas in the upper right corner up through the second hole down from the top and one mesh to the left of the right-hand side of the square. Secure the end of the thread in one of the two methods discussed in the box on page 15.

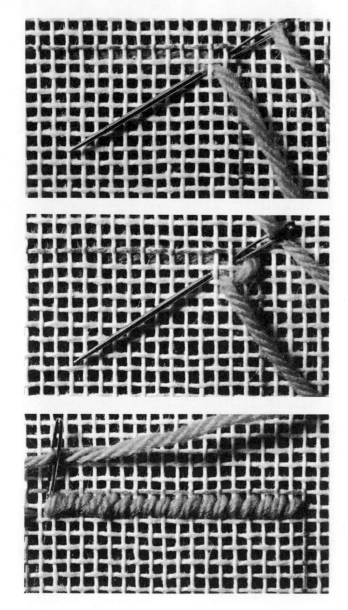

1. To take the first continental stitch, insert the needle one mesh to the right, one row above. Then with one motion bring the point of the needle up in the hole two meshes to the left and one row below. Pull needle and yarn through to the face of the canvas.

2. Repeat the same process for stitch number two: insert the needle in the hole one row above and one mesh to the right, then over to the hole two meshes to the left and one row below. Pull needle and yarn to the face of the canvas, and repeat the process, continuing to stitch the entire row until you reach the left-hand edge of the square marked on the canvas.

3. When you reach the last stitch of the row, do not continue the needle into the bottom of the next stitch. Instead, pull needle and yarn completely through to the underside of your canvas.

Continued on next page.

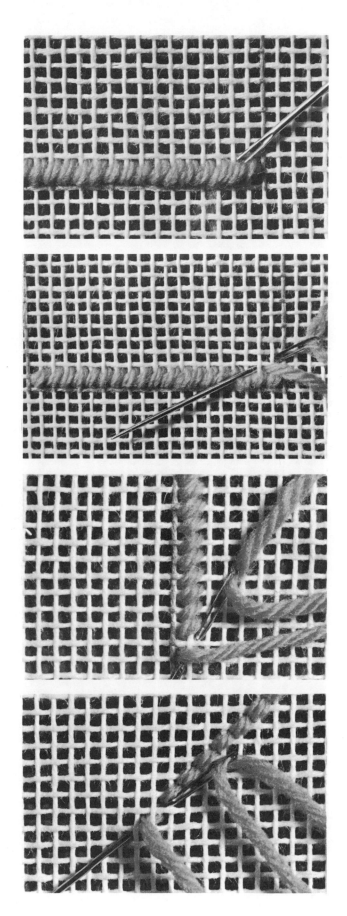

4. Rotate the canvas a half a turn (180°), and pull the needle up to the face of the canvas through what was the bottom of the second to the last stitch on row one. (The canvas is upside down; the first row of stitches is now on the bottom of the square.)

5. Repeat the stitching process for row two, beginning each new stitch from the top of the stitch on the row below. Always stitch a horizontal line of continental stitches from right to left.

If the yarn becomes tightly twisted while you are stitching, drop the needle end of the yarn, letting it dangle from the needlepoint piece until it stops turning. One method of avoiding this twisting is to roll the needle toward you every few stitches. As you gain experience in stitching, this process will come naturally.

6. Create a vertical line of continental stitches by working the stitches from top to bottom. Take one continental stitch, continuing the point of the needle down to the hole directly below the starting point (two rows below, one mesh to the left). Insert the needle one row above and to the right, then down to the hole directly below the starting point of the second stitch. After completing the row, rotate your canvas 180°, and work a second row from top to bottom.

7. A diagonal line of continental stitches is worked from upper right to lower left, all the stitches lying end-to-end. Take one continental stitch, and then continue the point of the needle to the hole one row below and to the left of your starting point. Insert the needle in the same hole as the base of your first stitch. Continue to the third stitch one row below and to the left of the second stitch. After completing the row of stitches, rotate your canvas 180°, working a second row from right to left. Finish the yarn end in one of the ways suggested in the box on page 15.

BASKETWEAVE is easy to work in large simple areas such as this leaf, a detail of sampler on page 22.

THE BASKETWEAVE STITCH

Using the same piece of canvas on which you practiced the continental stitch, mark off another 2-inch square with the indelible marker. Thread a needle, and begin a length of yarn in one of the two methods suggested in the box on page 15 (second method is used most often with the basketweave stitch).

The basketweave is different from the continental in that the rows are worked diagonally.

Note to left-handed workers: turn photographs upside down and reverse instructions. Work from left to right, bottom to top.

1. Starting in the upper right-hand corner of the square, pull the needle and thread to the face of the canvas two holes down from the top and one mesh to the left of the right side of the square. Take one continental stitch, and continue the needle point two meshes to the left and one row below. Pull needle and yarn to the face of the canvas.

2. Insert the needle one mesh to the right and one row above but continue the point of the needle into the hole two rows directly below. Pull needle and yarn to the face of the canvas.

3. Insert the needle into the hole one row above and one mesh to the right; then continue the needle into the hole two rows below, one mesh to the left — under the base of what will be the third stitch. Pull needle and yarn to the face of the canvas.

Continued on next page.

4. Insert the needle horizontally into the hole one row above and one mesh to the right and into the hole two meshes to the left in the same row. Pull needle and yarn through to the face of the canvas.

5. Insert the needle one row above, one mesh to the right and continue the point of the needle horizontally into hole two meshes to the left in the same row. Pull needle and yarn through to face of canvas.

6. Insert the needle one row above, one mesh to the right and continue two meshes to the left, one row below. Pull needle and yarn to the face of the canvas.

7. Insert the needle one mesh to the right and one row above, but continue the point of the needle vertically into the hole two rows directly below. Pull needle and yarn through to the face of the canvas.

Continued on next page.

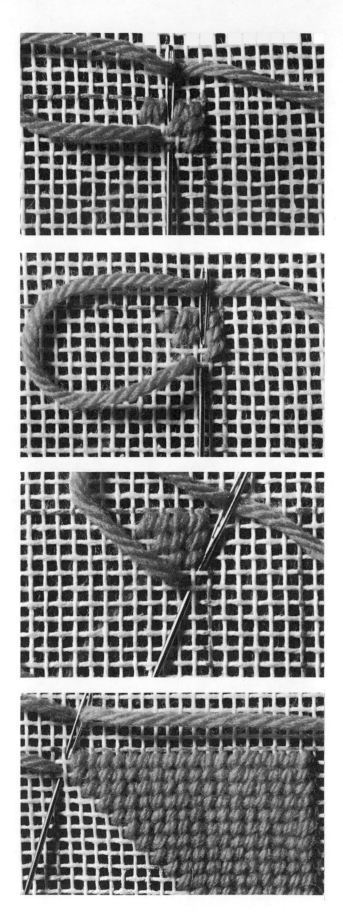

Continued from previous page.

8. Insert the needle one row above and one mesh to the right, then vertically into the hole two rows below. Pull needle and yarn to the face of the canvas.

9. Insert the needle one row above and one mesh to the right, then into the hole two rows below. Pull needle and yarn to the face of the canvas.

10. Insert the needle one row above and one mesh to the right, and continue it into the hole two rows below but one mesh to the left. Pull needle and yarn to the face of the canvas.

Be sure that the last or first stitch of a row is flush with the border of the square.

11. Insert the needle one row above and to the right. Continue the needle horizontally into the hole two meshes to the left in the same row. Pull needle and yarn to the face of the canvas.

Continue stitching "up" this diagonal row, always inserting your needle parallel to the *horizontal* canvas threads. Once you come back "down" a row, however, always insert the needle parallel to the *vertical* canvas threads. When you reach the left side of the square marked on the canvas, take two stitches in the upper left corner vertically. When you reach the right lower corner, though, take two stitches horizontally. The rows are now growing shorter so that they conform to the border of the square.

Remember *never* to stitch two rows going in the same direction because this will cause a very subtle diagonal mark to appear on the surface of your needlepoint. This situation most often occurs when you start with a new thread.

To prevent this error, look at the back of the canvas: if the threads of the row you stitched last are facing down (vertical), your last row was stitched from upper-left down to the lower right. (This is shown in the photograph at left, below.) Your next row should start at the bottom and be worked back up to the top. The back of the stitches of a row that was worked "up" (from lower right to upper left) will have horizontal threads as shown below.

Back view of row going down

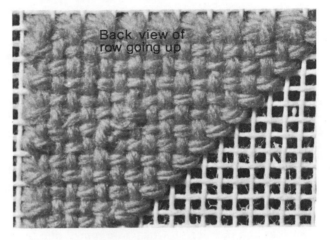

Back view of row going up

STITCHING IN BACKGROUND AREAS

Test your ability at working with a design and background by marking off a 2-inch square. Then draw a simple form in the center of this square. First, stitch the central design using basketweave.

The background can be worked one of two ways. The first method is to start in the right corner, working the basketweave down to the lower left corner. As you approach the central design, you can weave the yarn through the back of the center stitches to get to opposite sides.

Some disadvantages to this method are that the back of your piece becomes extremely bulky, yarn is needlessly wasted, and the stitches on the right side of the main design may become pulled and distorted. This method is best used when the central design is very small.

In the second method, the background portion is divided and worked separately. As a result, the thread is not woven through the central design. The picture on the right shows the different sections and the order in which they should be stitched.

Starting the background area in the right corner, work diagonal rows of basketweave just to the point where the stitching touches the top edge of the central design. Being careful not to stitch two rows in the same direction, start section B in the center of the right-hand side (begin from the point where you stopped section A). Begin section C in the center top of the square, making certain that you start the new row in the opposite direction from the end row of section A. Work the diagonal rows down to the left center of the design. Start section D at the center bottom of the square.

This order of stitching the background will assure you of never having two rows worked in the same direction.

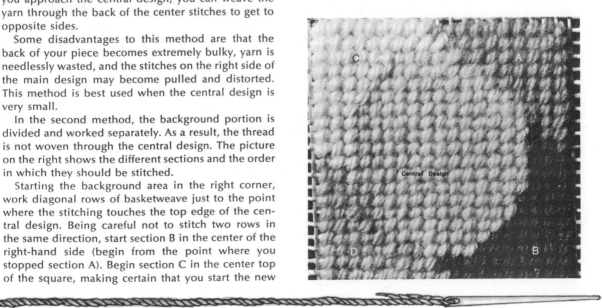

Decorative Stitches and Bargello Patterns

Painters have long tried to add depth and excitement to their paintings by creating differences in texture. To transfer paint onto canvas, they have laid aside their brushes and in their place have used palette knives. Nor have they stopped there in experimenting: some apply paint by dripping it onto the canvas; some try spraying it on; some even throw the paint — all in an effort to vary the texture.

The needlepointer, too, can create textural differences on his canvas. His technique for doing this is the decorative stitch.

Once you have mastered the basic stitches (continental and basketweave), you will want to know how to control the texture of your piece for a number of purposes. The few selected decorative stitches explained below, for example, are especially appropriate for wall hangings and pictures, in which tree trunks, hills, water, and other landscape details can be brought out effectively by decorative stitching. Even larger areas, such as entire backgrounds behind a design, can be worked in some simple decorative stitch — perhaps the Scottish or diagonal Parisian (see page 23 and 24).

Decorative stitches are often used for borders on pillows and other pieces. However, surfaces of chair seats, benches, footstools, and pillows that are often subject to hard wear should be worked with a sturdy stitch such as the basketweave. Basketweave produces a woven material that wears well; few stitches can match its strong and even texture.

Even though learning decorative stitching will make you a more versatile needlepointer, you should control the impulse to turn to it too frequently. Often too many decorative stitches in one piece merely clutter an otherwise excellent design. Used with restraint, though, and for a good reason, a decorative stitch can lead to elegant results.

Needlepoint's decorative stitches can be divided into three groups. These are discussed below: 1) stitches that cross meshes at a diagonal (the Scottish and diagonal Parisian stitches, page 23 and page 24); 2) textured or raised stitches (the cross and Smyrna stitches, page 26 and page 28); and 3) vertical or straight stitches (the Gobelin and brick stitches, page 29 and page 30). Included in the third group, Bargello (page 32) is a straight stitch but it is the overall pattern rather than the individual stitches that characterize it.

Although only a few of these decorative stitches have been used in the projects (pages 50-80), any of them can be substituted for the basketweave or continental with a few minor adjustments. (Remember: the

SAMPLER OF DECORATIVE STITCHES shows how effective different textures can be. (Also see inside front cover.)

graphed project patterns are based on each square representing one basic stitch. Many of the decorative stitches cover more than one mesh.) Practice the decorative stitches as you did the basic stitches, using a 2-inch square marked on mono canvas. To give a uniform appearance to your work, keep your yarn untwisted. Each stitch should be plump and round, not thin and flat. You will discover that the decorative stitches may require more yarn and thicker strands than the basic stitches. All the following stitches can be worked on mono canvas (12 or 14 mesh).

INTERESTING BACKGROUND STITCH, Scottish stitch is easy to do and quickly covers an area. See project on page 62.

THE SCOTTISH STITCH

The Scottish stitch is a small complete square composed of seven diagonally-taken stitches. The stitch begins with one small stitch over one mesh in the upper left-hand corner, then gradually increases to a stitch which covers at least four meshes in the center of the square. Different colors can be alternated with each complete row to produce a checkerboard pattern. The project on page 62 uses the Scottish stitch as a background pattern.

Practice the Scottish stitch in one of the 2-inch squares marked on your canvas. Within this square you might like to mark off several smaller squares (five meshes by five meshes) for the individual stitches.

Note to left-handed workers: no instruction change is necessary. Follow the directions given below.

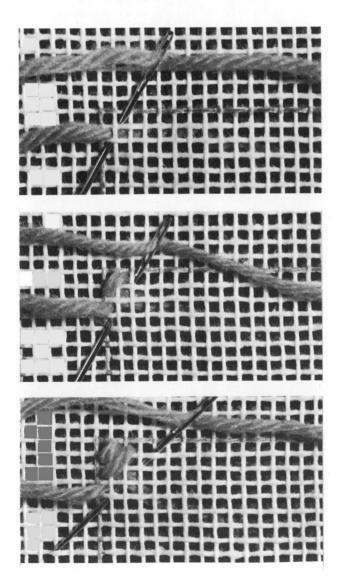

1. Begin a length of thread in one of the methods suggested on page 15. Bring needle and yarn to the face of the canvas through the second hole down from the upper left-hand corner of the 2-inch square. Insert the needle into the hole one row above and one mesh to the right. Continue the needle to the hole two rows down and one mesh to the left. Pull needle and yarn to the face of the canvas.

2. Insert the needle into the hole two meshes to the right and two rows above. Continue the needle to the hole two meshes to the left and three rows below, the hole directly below base of what will be stitch two. Pull needle and yarn to the face of the canvas.

3. Insert the needle three meshes to the right and three rows above. Continue the needle back three meshes to the left and four rows below. Pull needle and yarn to the face of the canvas.

Continued on next page.

Continued from previous page.

4. Insert the needle into the hole four rows above and four meshes to the right. Continue into the hole three meshes to the left, four rows below. Pull needle and yarn to the face of the canvas. You are now forming the opposite corner of the square by reducing the length of the diagonal stitches.

5. Insert the needle three rows above and three meshes to the right. Continue the needle two meshes to the left and three rows below. Pull needle and yarn to the face of the canvas. Insert the needle two meshes to the right and two rows above. Continue into the hole one mesh to the left and two rows below.

6. Pull needle and yarn to the face of the canvas, and complete the stitch by inserting the needle into the hole one row above and one mesh to the right. Continue the needle into the hole three rows down and one mesh to the left. You are now in position to begin the left top corner of the second Scottish stitch.

Experiment by alternating colors every other row of Scottish stitches to produce a checkerboard pattern.

THE DIAGONAL PARISIAN

The diagonal Parisian stitch is similar to basketweave in that the rows are worked diagonally, but the stitches alternate from a short stitch (over one mesh) to a long stitch (over two meshes). For variety, alternate colors every row or create subtle color changes by working each progressive row with a slightly darker or lighter hue of one color.

Note to left-handed workers: turn photographs upside down and reverse instructions. Work from left to right, bottom to top.

LIKE BASKETWEAVE, diagonal Parisian is worked in diagonal rows from upper left to lower right and back.

Continued on next page.

1. Begin the diagonal Parisian stitch in another 2-inch square marked on the canvas by starting a length of yarn in one of the methods suggested on page 15. Pull the needle and yarn to the face of the canvas in the hole one mesh to the left and three rows down from the upper right corner of the 2-inch square. Insert needle one row above and one mesh to the right, then continue to the hole one mesh to the left and two rows below. Pull needle and yarn to the face of the canvas.

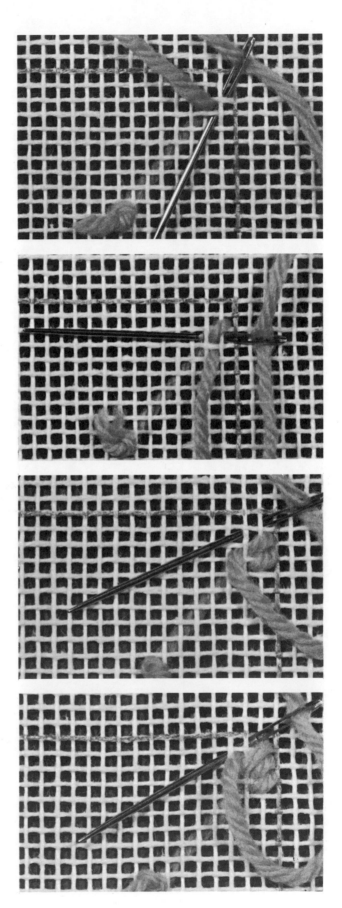

2. Insert needle one mesh to the right, one row above, and continue into hole two meshes directly to the left. Pull needle and yarn to the face of the canvas.

3. Insert needle two meshes to the right and two rows above. Continue needle two meshes to the left and one row below. Pull needle and yarn to the face of the canvas.

4. Insert the needle one row above and one mesh to the right, then continue to the hole one mesh to the left, one row below. Pull needle and yarn to the face of the canvas.

Continued on next page.

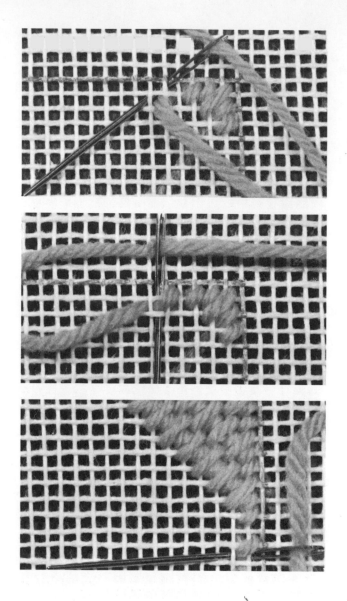

Continued from previous page.

5. Insert needle one mesh to the right and one row above, then continue needle over to the hole two meshes to the left, one row below. Pull needle and yarn to the face of the canvas and insert needle one mesh to the right and one row above. Continue needle into hole one mesh to the left and one row below. Pull needle and yarn to the face of the canvas.

6. Insert needle one row above and one mesh to the right. Continue needle two rows directly below. Pull needle and yarn to face of canvas. Insert the needle two meshes to the right and two rows above. Continue the needle down two rows below, one mesh to the left. Pull needle and yarn to the face of the canvas and insert needle one mesh to the right and one row above. Continue the needle into the hole two rows below, one mesh to the left. Pull needle and yarn to face of canvas.

7. Continue stitching down the row being certain that you alternate the short and long stitches. As you reach either side of the square, you will always execute two short continental stitches then skip one mesh and take two more short continental stitches before continuing up or down a row (see step 4). On a horizontal edge, the stitches will be taken horizontally; on a vertical edge, the stitches will be taken vertically.

THE CROSS STITCH

Once a very popular stitch, the cross stitch is rarely used today for anything more than small highlight areas in a needlepoint design. This stitch is formed by two diagonal stitches tilted in opposite directions. Because the cross stitch does not cover the canvas as well as either the basketweave or continental, work it loosely.

To do the cross stitch, begin in the upper right-hand corner of a 2-inch square marked on the canvas. The example that follows is worked over four meshes (four intersections or the equivalent area of four continental or basketweave stitches).

Note to left-handed workers: work from left to right using the same instructions below.

Continued on next page.

BEST IN SMALL AREAS, the cross stitch does not cover the canvas well but does create a lovely texture.

1. Use one of the methods of starting a thread shown on page 15. Bring needle and yarn from the underside to the face of the canvas through the third hole down from the top right corner of the square. Insert the needle two meshes to the left and two rows above; then continue it vertically down to the hole two rows below. Pull needle and yarn to the face of the canvas.

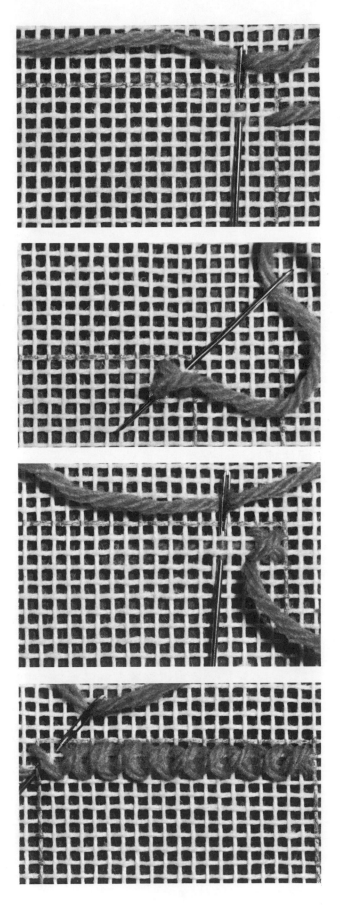

2. Insert the needle two rows above and two meshes to the right. Continue it back to the hole two meshes to the left and two rows below. Pull needle and yarn to the face of the canvas.

3. The next stitch is always started in the hole of the bottom left arm of the previous "x". Insert the needle two meshes to the left, two rows above, and back down to the hole two rows directly below. Pull needle and yarn to the face of the canvas.

4. Complete the second stitch by inserting the needle two rows above, two meshes to the right, and back down two rows below and two meshes to the left. Pull needle and yarn to the face of the canvas, and continue stitching.

Complete one row of cross stitches; but once you reach the left-hand border of the square, bring needle and yarn to the face of the canvas in the last stitch of the row.

Continued on next page.

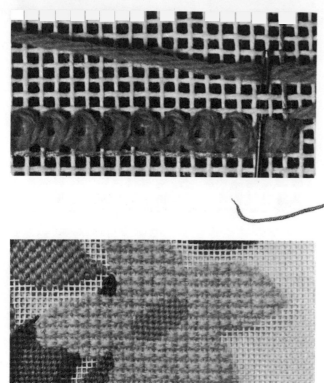

Continued from previous page.

5. Rotate entire canvas 180° as you did in the continental stitch. Repeat the stitching process to create a second row. Be sure that the top stitch of the "x" is always going in the same direction as you turn the canvas after each row.

THE SMYRNA STITCH

The Smyrna stitch is another textured stitch that can be executed over four meshes or more. Although the first two sections of the stitch are the same as the cross stitch, this stitch is easiest when worked from left to right. The instructions and photographs demonstrate two steps combined into one continuous movement. You might find it easier at first to take each step separately so that you alternate going through the face and the underside of the canvas.

Note to left-handed workers: no instruction change is necessary. Follow the instructions given below.

AN UNUSUAL TEXTURAL EFFECT can be created by using the Smyrna stitch, also called a "bump" stitch.

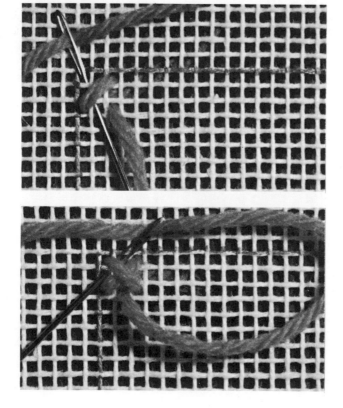

1. Start the Smyrna stitch in another 2-inch square marked on the canvas by beginning a length of thread in one of the methods suggested on page 15. Pull the needle and yarn to the face of the canvas three rows down from the upper left-hand corner of the 2-inch square. Insert the needle two rows above and two meshes to the right, and continue to the hole two rows below. Pull needle and yarn to the face of the canvas. Insert the needle into the hole two rows above and two meshes to the left. Continue the needle to the hole one mesh to the right and two rows below, between the bottom two "arms" of the "X". Pull needle and yarn to the face of the canvas.

2. Insert the needle into the hole two rows directly above. Continue into the hole one row down and one mesh to the left. Pull needle and yarn to the face of the canvas.

Continued on next page.

3. Insert the needle two meshes to the right in the same row. Continue the needle down to the hole directly below. Pull needle and yarn to the face of the canvas. You are now in position to begin the second Smyrna stitch.

Insert the needle two rows above and two meshes to the right, and repeat the same steps as for stitch number one. Complete one row; then rotate the canvas 180° to begin a second row.

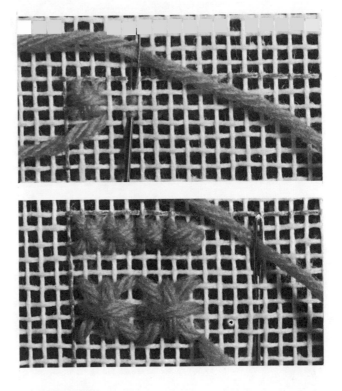

4. Worked over eight meshes, the stitch is much more visible and easier to execute. Because the bare canvas often shows between these stitches, some filling in may be necessary using the continental stitch.

THE UPRIGHT GOBELIN STITCH

Sometimes considered the vertical counterpart of the continental, the Gobelin stitch is easy to learn and goes quickly. Since Gobelin stitches do not cover the canvas as well as stitches taken diagonally across the meshes, don't pull the yarn too tightly as you work them. An example on page 77 shows the Gobelin used as a background stitch.

Note to left-handed workers: no instruction change is necessary. Follow directions given below.

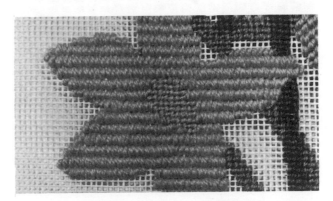

EASY TO LEARN and fast to work, the Gobelin stitch can be as large or as small as you like. See Bargello on page 32.

1. Begin the Gobelin stitch by securing the thread in one of the methods suggested on page 15. Then, starting from the upper left corner of a 2-inch square marked on the canvas, pull needle and yarn to the face of the canvas three rows below the left-hand corner of the square. Insert the needle into the hole two rows directly above. Continue the needle one mesh to the right and two rows below. Pull needle and yarn to the face of the canvas.

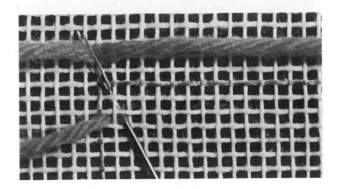

Continued on next page.

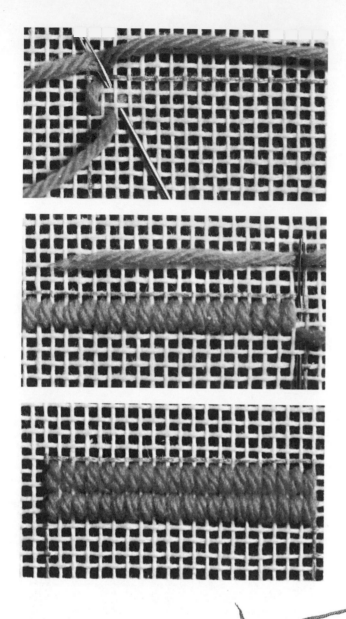

Continued from previous page.

2. Insert the needle two rows directly above and continue into hole two rows below, one mesh to the right. Pull needle and yarn to the face of the canvas.

3. Continue the stitching process until you complete the row to the border of the square. Then insert the needle two rows directly above, but continue the needle two rows below the bottom of the last stitch. Pull needle and yarn to the face of the canvas.

4. Insert the needle two rows above in the same hole as the bottom of the last stitch on row one, and continue the needle over one mesh to the left and two rows below. Continue stitching the second row from right to left.

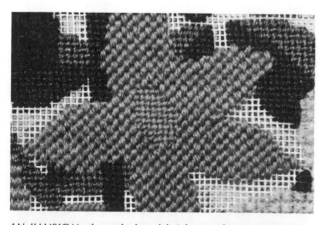

AN ILLUSION of neatly layed bricks can be created when you use the brick stitch in your needlepoint.

THE BRICK STITCH

Like the Gobelin, the brick stitch is worked up and down over at least two horizontal canvas threads. Since every other stitch is placed just one hole below the stitch next to it, a brick-like appearance is created. The brick stitch also resembles the continental stitch except that it is worked upright or straight.

Note to left-handed workers: no instruction change is necessary. Follow directions given below.

Continued on next page.

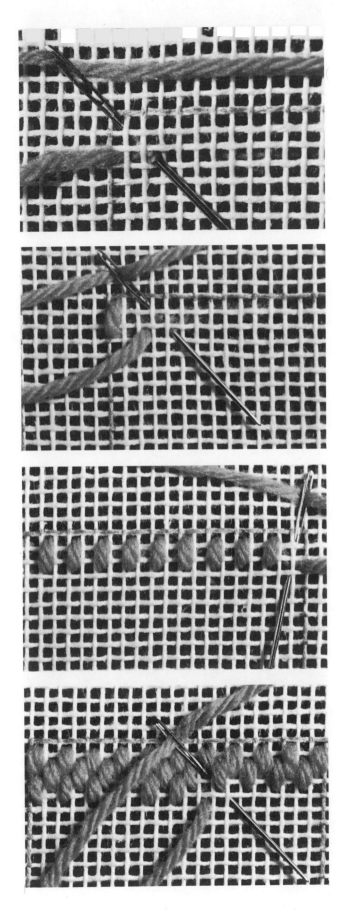

1. Start the brick stitch in a 2-inch square marked on the canvas. Secure the thread as suggested on page 15. Beginning in the hole three rows below the upper left-hand corner of the 2-inch square, take one Gobelin stitch, but continue the needle two meshes, rather than one mesh, to the right and two rows below. Pull needle and yarn to the face of the canvas.

2. Insert the needle two rows above, and continue to the hole two meshes to the right, two rows below. Pull needle and yarn to the face of the canvas.

3. Continue stitching to the right-hand border of the square. When doing the last stitch in this row, continue the needle from the top hole into the hole one mesh to the left and three rows below. Pull needle and yarn to the face of the canvas.

4. Insert the needle two rows above, and continue to the hole two meshes to the left, two rows below. Continue stitching the row. As you progress, notice how each stitch is taken slightly below and between the two stitches above. An actual brick design develops.

THE BARGELLO STITCH

Bargello has an old world flavor, a certain Renaissance magic. You will often find its characteristic repeat patterns in the upholstery on historical pieces of furniture. Yet every time someone attempts this simple stitch, a new repeat pattern emerges. The Bargello is actually a Gobelin-like stitch worked over any number of horizontal canvas threads, using any number of different colored yarns.

Bargello is characteristically made up of peaks, ridges, and geometric shapes, all produced by the sequence of the stitches. Its familiar patterns grow more from the choice of yarn color combinations, size and sequence of the stitches than from the actual technique of stitching. The following photographs show just a few suggested patterns that you can practice or use as inspirations in creating your own repeat designs.

Pattern number one

Stitch lengths: over two horizontal canvas threads and over six horizontal canvas threads.
Suggested colors in the order they were worked: royal blue, off-white, pale forest green, creamy beige, medium forest green, honey beige.

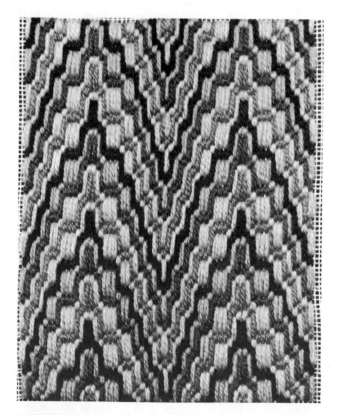

PATTERN ONE illustrates a typical Bargello pattern of peaks and valleys. (Also see inside back cover.)

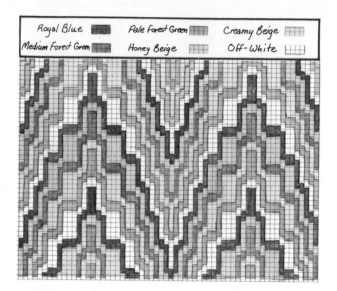

Royal Blue �, Pale Forest Green ▨, Creamy Beige ▦
Medium Forest Green ▨, Honey Beige ▦, Off-White ⫿

PATTERN ONE (CHART). Grid represents canvas threads. Use two stitch lengths: over 2 and 6 canvas threads

Like the Bargello pattern number three, the lines of stitches are a simple zigzag but with a stair-stepping effect that is created by alternating the stitch length every row.

Beginning with the royal blue and starting on the bottom right or bottom left of an area marked on the canvas, stitch a diagonal row up the canvas, making the stitches the length (over a certain number of horizontal canvas threads) and in the order as follows: 2,6,2,6,2,6,2,6,2,2,6,2,2,2,6,2. Take two long stitches (6,6) at the peak, then begin the diagonal row down, matching stitch lengths to the diagonal row going up. (See the graph above to determine how many canvas threads each successive stitch rises or descends.)

Continue the zigzag pattern across the area marked on your canvas. Start a second row of zigzags above the first using the next color suggested. The stitch lengths are just opposite what was taken in the row directly below. As one example: above a single stitch of blue worked over *two* horizontal canvas threads, a single stitch of off-white should be taken over *six* horizontal canvas threads.

Continue stitching a new color for each row, making sure that every other row follows the same stitching pattern.

Pattern number two

Stitch lengths: outline stitch—over two horizontal canvas threads; filler stitches—over 1,2,3,4,3,2,1 horizontal canvas threads (in both shades).
Suggested colors: orange outline, two shades of green for filler.

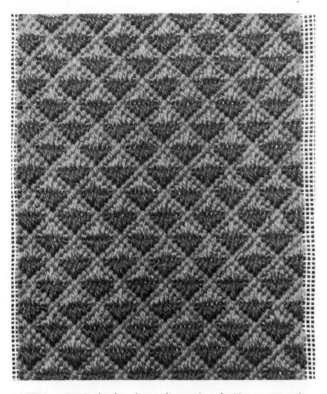

PATTERN TWO *looks three-dimensional. Use contrasting colors to create visual color vibration (see inside back cover).*

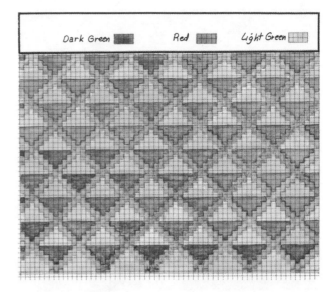

Dark Green ▨   Red ▦   Light Green ⊞

PATTERN TWO (CHART). *First establish the space between single diagonal lines, then fill in diamond centers.*

A suggestion of depth and dimensionality is created in this design by using two shades of a cool color and enclosing them with vivid bands of a bright contrasting color.

Begin in the upper right corner of an area indicated on your canvas and stitch a diagonal row of upright stitches to the lower left edge of the marked area. Each stitch covers two canvas threads and drops *down* one thread each succeeding stitch. When the first row is completed, count down ten horizontal canvas threads from the base of the last stitch. Begin your next diagonal row (lower left to upper right) in the hole below the tenth horizontal canvas thread. Stitch as directed for the first diagonal row, but take each successive stitch one canvas thread *above* the previous stitch. Once you reach the upper right side of the marked area, again count down ten horizontal canvas threads from under the base of the last stitch taken and begin your next descending diagonal row from the hole under the tenth horizontal canvas thread.

Continue to stitch the diagonal rows from upper right to lower left and back. Fill in the area above and below the first diagonal row. Be certain that each new diagonal row is started below or above the tenth horizontal canvas thread (for accuracy, count along the sides of the area to be stitched).

To create the diagonal rows running in the opposite direction, begin the first diagonal row in the upper right corner of the piece and stitch from the lower right edge to the upper left edge. Take the first stitch at the end of one of the existing diagonal rows. From this new diagonal line of stitches, slanting from lower right to upper left, you can begin spacing the rest of the diagonal rows. Count ten *vertical* canvas threads along the top edge and begin a second diagonal row (upper left to lower right) from the hole next to the tenth vertical canvas thread. Continue working the diagonal rows from upper left to lower right and vice versa. Be sure to count ten canvas threads before starting another diagonal row (to be accurate, count canvas threads along the side of the pattern).

A field of small diamonds should be produced by all the intersecting and evenly spaced diagonal rows.

When the diagonals are completed, divide each diamond in half horizontally to create an upper and lower triangle. Using the stitch pattern mentioned above, stitch the upper triangle in light green, the lower in dark green. Work one color at a time, stitching horizontally across the canvas.

Pattern number three

Stitch lengths: over four horizontal canvas threads.
Suggested colors in order of position: white, group 1 light, group 2 light, group 1 medium, group 2 medium, group 1 dark, group 2 dark.

This is the easiest pattern of all the Bargello examples because zigzag rows of alternating color are created by diagonal rows of stitches all the same size. Choose three graded values of one color (group 1) and

Continued on next page.

PATTERN THREE has stitches that are all the same size worked into peaks and valleys. (Also see inside back cover.)

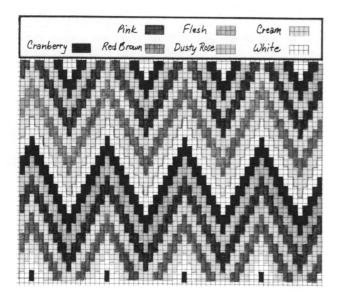

Pink	Flesh	Cream
Cranberry	Red Brown	Dusty Rose	White

PATTERN THREE (CHART). Work each stitch over 4 canvas threads; place stitches above or below previous stitch.

three graded values of another color (group 2). The white acts as accent.

Using the white yarn, begin the first row of zigzag across the bottom of the area marked on your canvas from the left or right edge. Work each stitch over four horizontal canvas threads. First take eight stitches *up* a diagonal row (each stitch sits two horizontal canvas threads above the previous stitch). Take a ninth stitch at the peak, then work eight more stitches *down* a diagonal row (each stitch sits two horizontal canvas

threads *below* the previous stitch) to a second point or ninth stitch.

Alternate row colors in the positions suggested above, building row upon row until the upper portion of the canvas is filled in. (The stitches in one row fall directly above the stitches of the previous row.)

When completing the bottom portion (under the first row you stitched), take your stitches directly *below* those of the previous row and continue until the piece is finished.

As you approach the upper and lower borders, it will be necessary to shorten the diagonal rows and eventually shorten the length of your stitches in order to end exactly on the edge you have marked.

Pattern number four

Stitch lengths: over two horizontal canvas threads.
Suggested colors: white, four values of blue (light to dark), four values of yellow (light to dark).

Creating an illusion of three-dimensionality and texture, this pattern of woven ribbons of color is the most difficult of the four Bargello designs shown. But once the spacing between diagonal lines is established, it merely requires a simple repetitive stitching sequence.

Beginning at the upper right-hand corner of an indicated area, start a diagonal row (from right to lower left) of upright stitches with the darkest blue yarn. Take eight upright stitches, dropping *down* one thread for each stitch taken. Continuing the diagonal row, skip four stitches, then take eight more stitches and repeat this sequence until you reach the opposite side of the indicated area. Count down ten horizontal canvas threads from the base of the last stitch. Begin a second diagonal row of dark blue in the third hole below the tenth horizontal canvas thread. Work back up to the upper right-hand corner skipping four stitches between each group of eight (each stitch is taken one canvas thread *above* the stitch below).

When ending one row and beginning another, it is best to tie off the yarn and begin the next row with a new strand to prevent any bulkiness from excessive yarn along the edges of the canvas.

Continue stitching diagonal rows of dark blue, spacing each row ten canvas threads apart (count along the edges for accuracy).

Once the dark blue lines are completed, you can begin stitching the three remaining colors of blue, working each lighter value of blue above the darker one and using it as a guide. The stitches in each new line of color are taken one canvas thread above the top of the stitch in the row before.

Beginning with the darkest yellow, fill in the open spaces (4 stitches wide) between the blue bands in the same manner as the blue diagonal lines but from upper left to lower right. First stitch the single diagonal lines using the darkest yellow, then fill in the three remaining yellow values on top (in the same value order as the blue). The yellow rows are stitched exactly like the blue: stitch eight, then skip four.

When all of the yellow diagonal lines are completed, fill in the remaining unworked areas with four upright stitches, each taken over two horizontal canvas threads (use creamy white yarn).

PATTERN FOUR simulates a basket weave. Gradation of colors creates three-dimensional bands (see inside back cover).

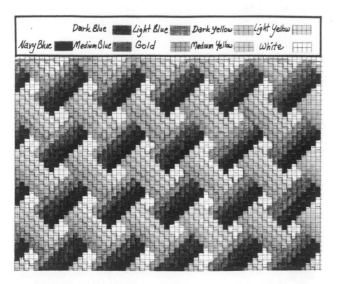

PATTERN FOUR (CHART). Establish spacing between diagonal lines, then work one color at a time.

BARGELLO, A BRIEF HISTORY

Take your choice of names—Bargello, Flame Stitch, Florentine canvas work, or Hungarian Point. This labeling confusion is part of the fascination of the stitch, because it reflects the enigma of its origins.

Many stories exist concerning the history of Bargello, most of them quite romantic. Tapestry weaving stitches (upright stitches), similar to what we now call Bargello, were used by the Egyptians, Babylonians, Greeks, and Romans.

More recent Bargello development has two groups of partisans: the Florentine school and the Hungarian theorists. The "Bargello" is a museum in Florence (now called the Museo Nazionale), formerly a jail for political prisoners as well as the residence of the chief magistrate. One story tells of condemned prisoners whiling away their time by needlepointing complex designs, but actually each person was confined only a few days before his execution took place. Hardly time enough to construct intricate needlework! However, the museum does contain four 17th century chairs done in Florentine canvas work. This may explain the association of the term Flame Stitch with the word Bargello, as these chairs are extremely fine examples of the style. (Flame stitch has the characteristics of an actual flame with a gradation of yarn colors from dark to light.) Adding to the confusion, the Museo Nazionale inventory specifies its famous chairs to be *punto unghero* (Hungarian Point) silk embroidery. One authority simplified the matter by stating that the stitching technique was popular in Florence, so acquired the name of the city.

In the 15th century, Florence was the main center of embroidery in Italy. Important painters such as Botticelli, Paolo Veronese, and Alvise Vivarini designed embroideries executed with silk thread in brick stitch, the stitch from which Bargello probably developed.

Florentine needlework became more stately and ecclesiastical in the 16th century and was designed to be seen from a distance, perhaps leading to use of heavier yarns and the striking patterns of Bargello.

Hungary is particularly famous for its wide variety of colorful folk embroideries. Early Hungarians probably learned geometric stitching from their contact with the Turks. Proponents of Hungarian origins of the Hungarian stitch have an answer for the development of the term "Bargello". Around 1383, a Hungarian princess who loved needlework was married to a Polish king of the Jagiello family, also spelled Jagello. Perhaps "Bargello" is a variation of this name.

Hungarian Queen Maria Teresa, in the 18th century, was a Hungarian Point enthusiast and introduced the study of needlework into Hungarian schools. Much exchanging of designs between countries was carried on by schoolgirls until the middle of the 18th century.

Wherever it originated, Bargello canvas stitching is now popular everywhere. Today the beautiful, mysterious style can be used to create new designs rivaling the famous chairs in the Bargello.

Working a First Project from Start to Finish

Having mastered the techniques of needlepoint stitching, you will feel ready to "solo." If you have built up a great deal of confidence at this point, the sky's the limit. But if you would like to test your stitching ability a bit more before designing your own piece, a pre-designed canvas or a needlepoint kit may be in order.

Some professionally-designed canvases have a complete design painted onto them; others come with the central motif completely stitched in, leaving only the background area for you to stitch.

Needlepoint kits usually include a pattern painted on canvas and the necessary amount of yarn. Thus the preliminary steps of buying canvas, choosing a pattern, transferring it to canvas, and estimating the correct amount of yarn needed are reduced to one step. When purchasing a kit, though, check carefully to be certain that its canvas and yarn are of good quality.

Many needlepointers use kits because they feel they have no designing or drawing ability. Yet you do not have to be an artist to come up with a successful idea. Most needlepoint designs are inspired by the things around us: printed curtains, rugs, posters, calendars, postcards, magazine clippings, children's coloring books, clothing material, business logos, or photographs of vegetables or fruits. All of these can easily be traced and transferred onto a canvas.

When it comes to choosing a design, the only limitation is your imagination. Of course, you must be careful when deciding upon a design not to choose one that has tightly-curved patterns or elaborate detail. Until you become quite proficient, work with fairly simple and bold patterns. Too much detail may require some petit point, and unless you are a patient person, such fine stitching may make your first project less satisfying than it could be.

STEPS IN CREATING YOUR FIRST NEEDLEPOINT PROJECT

As an example of a possible first piece, a pillow has been chosen to illustrate the basic techniques, from the first step of selecting a design to actually finishing the project (see front cover and photograph at right). Designing and creating a needlepoint pillow has these advantages: it lends itself well to any design you might choose, and the basic finishing process can be adapted to most needlepoint pieces you might make in the future. Use this chapter as a step-by-step guide to completing your own pillow of the same design, or use

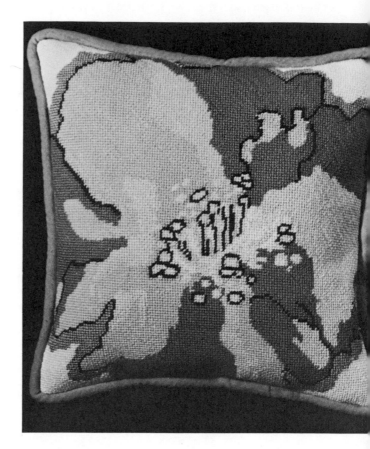

A KNIFE-EDGED PILLOW is a good first needlepoint project to attempt. See cover for color view of unfinished design.

it as a general reference for procedures in making any needlepoint project.

Choosing a design and yarn colors. Your first concern is to find a design for your needlepoint piece. Certain limitations should guide you when making the choice. If there are any curved forms in your design, they will not have a perfect edge when reproduced in needlepoint. As demonstrated in the design at right, you can only stitch over the meshes closest to the outline. Small circles and curves may be impossible to reproduce in stitching when using mono canvas 14 mesh or less. The fewer canvas threads to the inch the more you must execute your tight curves as squares and angles. Using Penelope canvas, however, you can combine petit point stitches with the gros point and achieve the details and curved shapes.

Keep in mind that you are not trying to reproduce your design photographically into needlepoint. You are re-interpreting the idea onto the canvas, giving the design a completely different feeling. If you are a beginner, try to avoid fine details and extensive shading. The best designs to work with are large, flat, and uncluttered. When choosing a design, take into account the shape or border of the finished piece. This will allow you to position your design effectively on the canvas.

Having decided on a design, you will next consider the colors to express it in. If you take your idea from a colored picture, you can use the same colors, or you can substitute your own color scheme. Wool yarns are available in such a broad spectrum of hues that it is difficult to limit yourself to only a few colors. But the fewer colors you work with at first, the easier it will be to concentrate on the design and the mechanics of stitching.

One good method of choosing colors is to refer to a "color wheel". On the color wheel, the colors are placed in a circular formation, showing those that are complementary to each other or those that will combine pleasingly. Complementary colors are orange with blue, yellow with violet, or red with green. Many references are available if you would like to study color theories more thoroughly.

Another successful method of combining color is to use several different shades of one color, such as navy blue, medium blue, and pale blue. You could also rely primarily on your own judgment: what is a pleasing color combination to you? Where and with what will your finished piece be used? Examine your clothing and how you coordinate certain accent accessories with your outfit. Looking outside yourself, notice the color combinations that other people use in their dress or their homes. Observe the delicate color combinations so frequently found in nature, for example, the soft color transitions in the petals of a rose. Color combinations, like design possibilities, are constantly being suggested around you.

Choosing your materials. The amount of detail in your design will determine the gauge of canvas you should choose. A number 12 mono canvas was picked for the pillow design because of the simplicity and bold lines of the flower. A number 18 needle with two-strand Persian wool was selected to cover the number 12 canvas well. Backing for the pillow is a soft velveteen, color coordinated with the pattern. A polyester stuffing and unbleached muslin were used to make the inner pillow.

Preparing the canvas. Cut the canvas so that you will have at least a two to three-inch margin around the edge of your entire piece. (If you want the pillow to be 12 inches by 12 inches, cut a piece of canvas 15 by 15 inches square.) Not only is this convenient when blocking your needlepoint but also it gives you extra working space in case you want to extend your design slightly after the project is underway.

Mask all the edges of canvas with tape (one-inch masking tape), or fold over the raw edges and baste securely. Finishing the edges prevents the canvas threads from raveling and creates a smooth edge so that your yarn will not catch as you stitch.

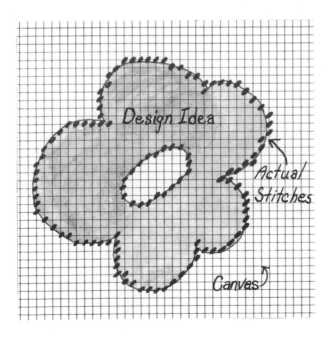

STITCHES CAN ONLY be taken over the mesh nearest the outline of a design. Curves become a series of steps.

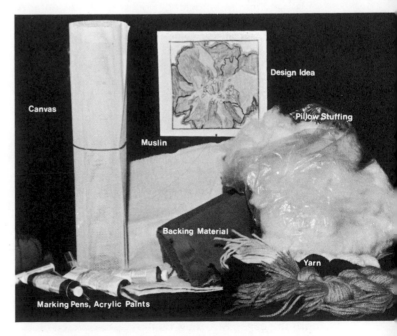

FEW MATERIALS are needed to construct a pillow. Choose them carefully, keeping pillow design and colors in mind.

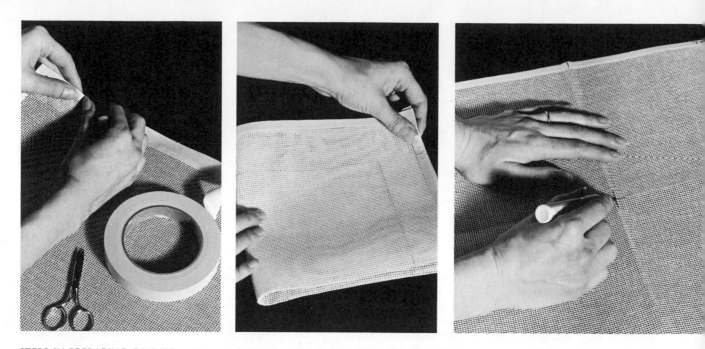

STEPS IN PREPARING CANVAS: cut canvas 2-3 inches larger than pillow dimensions, bind edges with masking tape, fold to find center, then mark exact center in the middle of the canvas and along the edges. Indicate "top" of canvas, as well.

A good idea: mark the top of your canvas so that, if you turn it at any time, you will not make the error of turning it just 90° (¼ of a circle) and stitching in the wrong direction. When using Penelope canvas, be sure that the threads closest together are the vertical (or up and down) threads. To assure this, the selvage of the canvas should be on the side.

To facilitate the blocking process, find the center of each side of the canvas. Fold the canvas in half horizontally, then in half again vertically. Mark the center points on the edge and the face of your canvas with an *indelible* marking pen. To indicate the exact center of your canvas, mark a "+" (see photographs above).

The mark in the center of the canvas helps you to place the design and center the outline of the pillow shape. Count the meshes from this center point to determine the edges of your pillow; mark them with an *indelible* pen. Because this pillow is 12 inches by 12 inches, 72 meshes were counted on each side of the center mark (remember 12 mesh canvas has 12 stitches to the inch). Draw the border line of the pillow starting from the center to the 73rd mesh on all four sides (see photograph top left, opposite page).

On a paper-covered board (brown wrapping paper or tinfoil) to be used later as a support for blocking, mark the outline of the entire piece of canvas. Indicate on the paper the same center markings that you put on the edges of the canvas (see photograph top right, opposite page). Also draw on the paper-covered blocking board, the outline of the pillow. When you block the piece, these marks will be used to line up your

canvas. After you have worked the needlepoint, the marks on the canvas and board will undoubtedly no longer line up. You will have to pull at the damp canvas until these marks correspond (this is discussed further in process of blocking, page 42).

Transferring a design. An old Chinese proverb says, "A journey of 1,000 miles begins with a single step." The first steps of your needlepoint project are behind you when you have bought the materials, prepared the canvas for needlework, and chosen the design. If the design happens to be the correct size for your pillow, so much the better.

The next easy step is to make a tracing of the design, simplifying or adjusting the lines until it is appropriate for needlepoint. After you lay the tracing under the canvas, draw the design onto the canvas with an *indelible* marker (see page 13). For easier reading, tape the design to a window which has light coming through it, and hold the canvas over it as you trace. Ignoring the mesh formation of the canvas, follow the lines of the design. You will determine the actual placement of stitches once you begin working. If your yarn colors are light, use a light-colored *indelible* ink for the outline. (A black or dark ink will produce shadows under light-colored yarn.)

One of the most convenient methods of transferring a design is to apply a pre-designed iron-on image, the kind often used for embroidery. A package of several different images costs little and can be purchased in five and dime stores as well as in needlework shops.

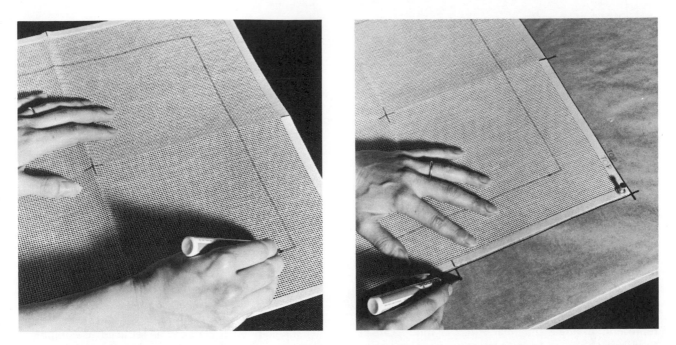

COUNTING MESHES from center of canvas, determine the border of the pillow. Place canvas on the paper-covered blocking board and mark pillow outline, canvas outline, and all the center marks that appear on the edge of the canvas.

Follow the directions given on the package for easy application of the design.

Once you transfer the design onto canvas, you can either begin your stitching or go one step further to simplify the needlepoint work. The additional step of coloring in the design on the canvas with acrylic paints creates an accurate color guide to follow as you stitch. Use paint colors about the same shades as your yarn and carefully plan the color scheme on the paper tracing of your design before you begin painting.

Acrylic paints are simple to use because they are water soluble. You do not have to be adept at painting in order to color in the design successfully. Just thin the paints with water until they are like a thick cream, and then apply the paint with a fine water-color brush until all the different color areas are covered but not saturated with paint (see photograph at right). Let the paint dry thoroughly before you begin working on the canvas.

The greatest advantage in working with a painted canvas is that you need to concentrate less intently on your work. You can enjoy listening to the radio, watching television, or carrying on a conversation as you stitch. Another advantage of a painted canvas is that it conceals areas not covered completely by the yarn. This is especially helpful when using any vertical decorative stitches (see page 29) because the bare canvas is often visible between the individual stitches. On the other hand, the painted surface can make it difficult to see the holes in which you should take stitches or the areas where you may have forgotten some stitches as you worked.

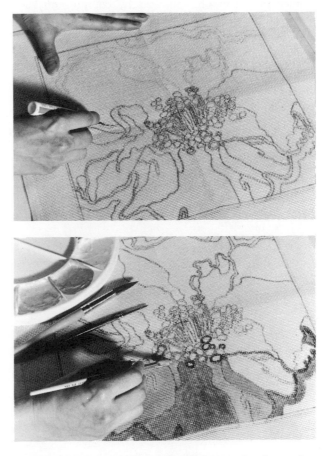

TRANSFERRING A DESIGN to the canvas can be done using an indelible pen and/or acrylic paints.

Graphing a design. Rather than working on a painted canvas, some needlepointers prefer a "blank" canvas with a graphed rendition of their design as a separate guide. You may prefer this exacting method, even though it requires complete concentration.

To begin graphing, lightly trace your design onto a piece of graph paper (paper having ten squares to the inch is the most standard measure carried in stationery stores). Remember: if you are working on any canvas size other than 10 mesh, the design drawn on 10 squares to the inch graph paper will be larger than the design worked on canvas 12 mesh or more, and smaller than the design worked on canvas 8 mesh or less. Working on petit point canvas (twenty stitches to the inch), as one example, your design drawn on 10 to the inch graph paper will be *twice* the size of your finished petit point piece. (See graph and finished piece on page 69.)

Begin "squaring" the edges of the design that you transferred onto the graph paper to conform to the squares of the grid (see photograph below). Each square represents a single diagonal stitch. Symbols can be used in each square to indicate colors: for instance, a dot could represent blue, a diagonal line could represent yellow, and so forth, or the areas can be lightly colored with crayons or colored pencils. Constant reference to the graph, followed by counting off each stitch on the canvas, is tedious but necessary. Using a graph, though, assures exactness of design in any geometric or repetitive pattern. Graphs are particularly useful when you wish to stitch numerals or letters onto your canvas (see box on page 76).

One other graphing method (below, at right) is not so much an accurate guide as a general indication of where stitches will be placed. Once the design has been traced onto the graph paper, the second step of "squaring" the edges is unnecessary. Each intersection of two lines (rather than a square) indicates a single diagonal stitch. The graph paper actually represents the canvas mesh. Since symbols for the colors would only confuse the design, it is much simpler to fill in the color areas with colored pencils or crayons.

The advantage of this type of graph is that the actual placement of stitches can be decided upon as you stitch. If you plan to use any decorative stitches (pages 22–35) — those that are often worked over more than a single mesh — you can make allowances as you work. The graph does not limit you to a certain number of stitches in any given area. Although this second method is less restricting, it too requires you to constantly refer from the graphed design to the canvas and back.

All patterns for projects included later in the book (pages 48–80) are illustrated using the first type of graph explained above. However, if you wish to substitute different stitches for the ones suggested in each project, the graphed designs can be retraced and simplified into a chart by means of the second method discussed above. Or if you should want to have a photo copier enlarge or reduce the pattern to a different size from that shown in the project so you can trace the design directly onto your canvas, the suggested size enlargement or reduction is always indicated in the directions for the project (a discussion of reducing and enlarging a design follows).

Graphing a design either way allows you to make adjustments on paper rather than on your canvas. This way you are also better able to visualize how the image will look once it is needlepointed. Because fitting a

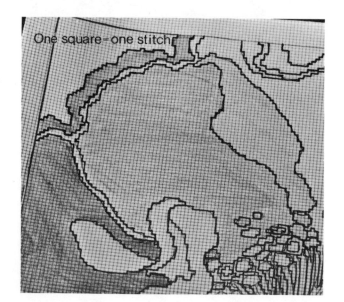 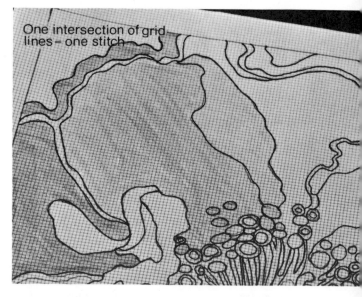

CHARTING THE DESIGN ON PAPER, you can work on a blank canvas and count off stitches. In graph at left, each square represents one stitch. In graph at right, each intersection of a horizontal and vertical line represents a stitch.

design into the confines of a grid pattern makes you aware of elements to look for in future designs, some people feel that graphing provides excellent training for the beginning needlepoint enthusiast.

Both graphing methods discussed above are possible if the design chosen is the correct size. But what do you do if the design is too small or too large for the pillow?

Reducing and enlarging a design. One of the simplest methods for reducing or enlarging a picture is to take it to a professional photo copier. This service can be found in a telephone book's yellow pages listed under ''photo-copying'' or ''blue print services.''

If the design you have chosen is a black and white picture with gray tones or a color picture, ask for a positive print enlarged or reduced to the scale you would like. Although the quality of the enlargement often is not perfect, it will be clear enough to trace from. The cost will vary, but on an average you will pay $4.50 because a negative as well as a print must be made. Price will also depend on the size of the enlargement or reduction of your design.

An alternative to the positive print is a line stat. To order a line stat, first make an accurate tracing of your design with a fine line pen. Then give the tracing to the photo copier and ask for a line stat enlarged or reduced to the scale you need. This can cost as little as $2.00. So if indications of shading and gray areas are not necessary to understanding your design, you can save money by ordering a line stat instead of a positive print (see examples at right).

If no photo-copying services are available in your community, it's easy to adjust the design to the correct size yourself. Trace the original design onto a piece of paper that has been marked in a grid pattern of from ¼-inch squares to 1-inch squares or more, depending on the size of your original design (see illustration at right). On another piece of paper, draw a second grid pattern. Make the squares of this either larger or smaller than those on the first sheet — larger if you are increasing the image, smaller if you are reducing it. Copy the design from each block of the first grid onto the corresponding block of the second grid, enlarging or reducing it, as the case may be. One example of this process: if you superimpose your original design on a grid of 1-inch squares and wish to enlarge the image two times, mark off a second grid with 2-inch squares, and redraw the design on the larger grid (see illustration at right). The drawing will not be an accurate reinterpretation but will be close enough to use as a pattern for your graph or canvas.

Beginning to stitch. With the design transferred to your canvas or graph, you are prepared to begin your needlepoint. Choose a comfortable chair with good lighting, and place scissors and a supply of yarn close by. To begin, study your canvas and design; determine which areas should be done first and where any future problems might exist. A good approach is to always

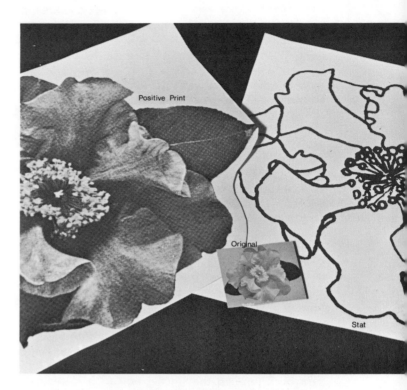

POSITIVE PRINT enlargement (left) or line stat enlargement (right) can easily be traced onto your canvas.

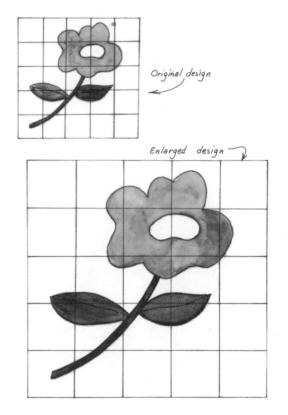

ENLARGE THE DESIGN by yourself. Draw a grid over original design, then transfer it to a larger grid.

begin in the center and stitch out to the edges. Always work main images and lines before you fill in the background. Don't hesitate to turn your canvas as much as needed to get to inaccessible areas. But remember always to rotate the canvas 180° so that all your stitches are slanting in the same direction and do not work two successive rows of basketweave in the same direction.

To start your first thread, refer to the two methods explained on page 15. Then, holding the canvas in whatever position is most comfortable for you, begin stitching. (Most needleworkers prefer rolling two of the canvas edges so that only the area to be worked is exposed. This makes it much easier to hold the bulky canvas as you stitch.) As you use up a length of yarn, secure the end, and clip it close to the back of the canvas so you will keep the back neat, preventing the possibility of becoming tangled in loose yarn ends. As you tie off ends, weave the needle and thread at right angles to the row being worked. This prevents distortion on the face of the stitches.

If you should have to tear out a mistake, first pull the yarn out of the needle, and then carefully pick out each stitch, alternating from the face of the canvas to the underside. Do not try to weave the needle and yarn back through the stitches you wish to remove. This will only split threads and produce tangles.

If a large area of stitches must be removed, the quickest method is to cut them out. Slipping your small scissors under the stitches on the face of your canvas, cut very carefully to avoid slicing through the canvas threads (see photograph below). Pick out the cut ends until you come close to the point at which you want to stop. Pull out the last few stitches without cutting the yarn; then re-thread the yarn end, and secure it by weaving it into the back of the stitches. Be sure to secure the yarn end from where you began cutting the stitches. Any long lengths of yarn that have been pulled out should be discarded because the yarn is often worn too thin to cover the canvas well.

Blocking your needlepoint. Before doing any finishing on your piece, you will probably need to block it. If the canvas has not been severely misshapen, you can simply steam iron it slightly to improve the horizontal and vertical lines and to even out the stitches. Before ironing, cover the needlepoint with a protective damp cloth. Holding the iron just slightly above the piece, pull the needlepoint as you move the iron over it; straighten the edges as much as possible. This method is ideal for small items such as jewelry or buttons.

For larger pieces, blocking with the use of some moisture is recommended. Take the paper-covered board on which you traced the original outline (see

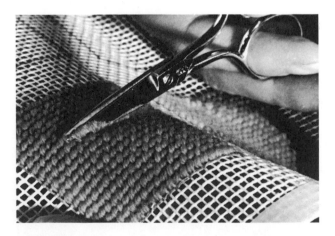

MISTAKES can be cut out. Be careful not to cut the canvas threads; weave back any loose yarn ends.

DISTORTION OF A PIECE is remedied by moistening it and tacking it onto the blocking board until dry.

page 39) of the now-completed canvas. By placing the stitched canvas on this outline, you can see how extreme the diagonal pull of the canvas has become. With a mixture of white vinegar and water (2-3 tablespoons of vinegar to 1-2 cups of water), sponge both sides of the canvas until the entire piece is wet, but not saturated. The vinegar and water mixture "sets" the yarn colors and helps prevent any possible running of the paint or ink you used in transferring the design onto the canvas. Place the needlepoint face down and begin tacking it to the board with aluminum or non-rusting tacks. Start tacking 1 inch away from the edge and in the center of each side of the stitched portion. Pull the piece as you tack until the canvas and stitched portion conform to the shape of the outlines on your board. Continue pulling and tacking around the canvas until there is approximately one tack for every inch or half inch. Do not tack into the needlepointed portion; if you do, visible indentations will remain on the face of your piece when it has dried. A draftsman's triangle placed along the edges of the stitched portion will help you determine when the needlepoint is correctly aligned.

Place the board and tacked canvas in a warm, dry spot. Let it remain horizontal for a period of 24-48 hours or until it is completely dry. You should notice at once that the stitches have evened out. If, after you remove the canvas from the board, the needlepoint insists in pulling into a diagonal position again, repeat the blocking process. If the continental stitch is used extensively in a piece, several blockings, along with a thin coating of rabbit skin glue on the back, may be necessary to keep the piece from slipping again. (Glue can be purchased at art supply stores and needlework shops.)

An alternate method of blocking a piece is to position it on the board dry, tack as if it were wet, then sponge it until it is thoroughly wet. Some find this method much more satisfactory.

Certain needlepoint canvases may require the hand of a professional blocker. To have a piece blocked in a needlepoint store can be expensive, but the cost may seem small when you consider the number of hours you may have spent making it. However, most needleworkers are quite able to block their own canvases. A suggestion: to get the feel of it, first try your hand at blocking a small piece of work.

MOUNTING AND FINISHING NEEDLEPOINT

Whatever needlepoint project you begin — pillow or eyeglass case, pincushion or wall hanging — will need mounting and finishing in the final stages. But not all pieces call for the same finishing process.

To help in finishing many of your projects, some techniques are explained below. Certain items, such as shaped handbags, large upholstered objects, or anything bound in leather, should be finished by a profes-

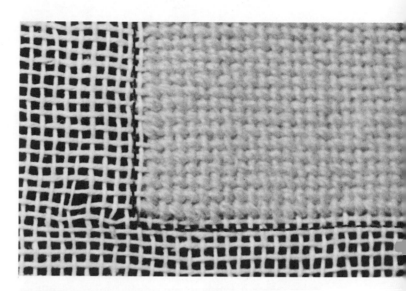

PREVENT CANVAS RAVELING by machine stitching around needlepointed section, then trim excess canvas along edges.

sional. Most needlework stores offer this service or can refer you to people who can professionally complete your piece.

After blocking your needlepoint, the edges of the canvas will be your major concern. How do you keep them from raveling? How do you turn under the edges and mount or line the piece? How do you miter a corner? These and other related questions are answered in the following discussion of finishing processes.

Preparing the canvas edges. Before beginning the finishing, machine stitch a couple of rows around the needlepointed section of the canvas as close as possible to the completed work without stitching into the needlepoint. Doing this will help to prevent the canvas from raveling as you work with it (see photograph above).

Backing needlepoint. If your needlepoint is to be backed so that it can be made into a knife-edged pillow or pincushion, cut a piece of closely-woven cloth (corduroy, velvet, felt, leather, or cotton duck) the same size as the canvas. Place the right sides of the cloth and the needlepoint together, and machine stitch a seam on three edges. Sew directly into the edge row of needlepoint because the bare canvas will not hold the stitching as well. Trim the backing and canvas to within one inch or less from the edge of the needlepointed section, depending on the size of the piece.

Turn the needlepoint casing so that the right side is out, and insert a ready-made pillow of the same size. (If no ready-made pillows of the correct size are available, make a pillow from inexpensive material and stuff it with dacron or kapok.) Once the inner pillow is inserted, use a blind stitch to close the fourth edge of the pillow, or add a zipper to permit easy removal of the needlepoint cover.

Edging for needlepoint. To give a more finished look to a piece of needlepoint, an edging of some type is often desirable. Provide for this by purchasing cotton welting or fringe that matches the color of your lining or backing material, or construct welting from a bias strip of the backing material and a length of cording. (Most general sewing guides contain directions for making welting.)

Place the welting inside the edge of the needlepoint. With the loose ends of the welting facing out and the rolled edge facing towards the needlepoint, baste the welting in place (see photograph below). Place the right sides of the backing and needlepoint together, and sew a seam on three sides of the pillow into the needlepoint, welting, and backing material. Use the zipper foot attachment of your sewing machine to stitch the pillow seams. On the fourth side, machine stitch only the welting to the needlepoint.

Turn the entire piece right side out. Insert the pillow, and blind stitch the fourth side of the backing to the welting (see photograph below) or stitch a zipper into the open end.

Working a binding stitch along the edges of the needlepointed section is another method of edging a project. Cut the corners of the canvas as explained for mitering (method 1, opposite page). Then fold the four edges of the canvas to the back of the needlepoint. Match the mesh, but leave at least one row of unworked canvas beyond the finished edge of needlepoint (see illustrations A and B below).

Starting in a corner, work the Gobelin (page 29) or continental stitch (page 16) along this unstitched edge of canvas. The width of this edging depends on the number of unworked rows you fold beyond the needlepoint. When you reach a corner, the stitches are taken through three thicknesses (see illustration C).

Once the edge is completely bound, you can attach a backing. Cut the backing slightly larger than the bound needlepoint. Turn under the edge of the backing; then place the wrong sides of the backing and needlepoint together. Blind stitch the turned under edge of backing just under the row of Gobelin stitches on three edges (see illustration D below). Insert the inner pillow, and stitch the fourth edge closed.

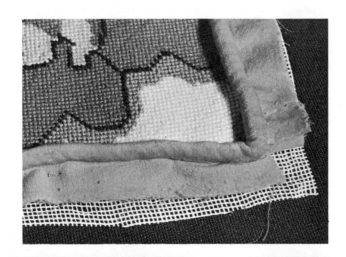

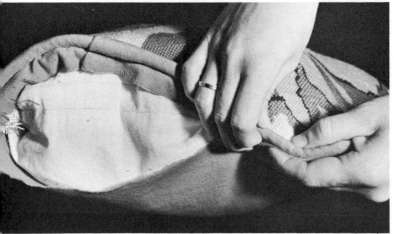

WELTING is attached along needlepointed section, backing is sewn on, then the inner pillow is inserted.

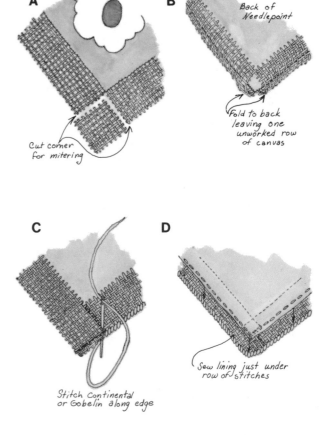

BIND EDGES of needlepoint by folding canvas edge and stitching row of Gobelin stitches on doubled-over canvas.

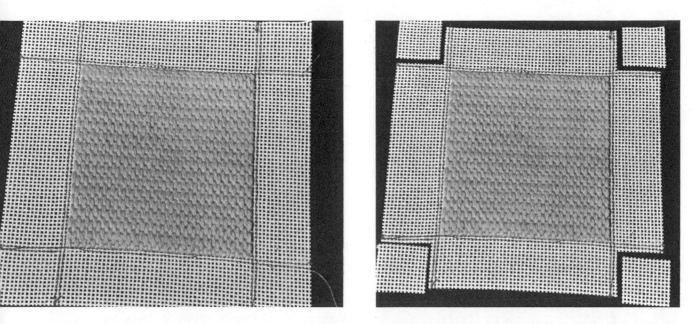

TO MITER CORNERS, first machine stitch along the needlepointed section to each edge of the canvas. Cut out the corners along stitching, creating a right angle space. Follow directions given below for two different methods of mitering.

An edging can also be attached after the needlepoint casing is filled with a pillow and closed on all four sides. To do this, crochet a single chain with a strand of matching yarn. Attach the braid with clear nylon thread along the seam of the backing and needlepoint.

Mitering corners. If your needlepoint is to be a hanging or anything that will lie flat, it will be necessary to miter the corners. Following the same beginning procedure as for constructing a pillow, machine stitch around the needlepoint, but stitch to each edge of the canvas so that right angles are formed in each corner (see photograph above). Trim the canvas to within 1 to ½ inch of the needlepointed section (less for smaller pieces). At each corner, cut just outside the stitching, and remove the canvas corner (see photograph above).

Once the corner has been cut out, it can be mitered by one of two methods: 1) fold the top canvas edge down and the side canvas edge in so that one edge lies on top of the other at the corners. Stitch the two edges together at each corner; or 2) fold back the two edges at the corner to form a diagonal corner, pulling the edges to the back of the canvas and stitching the corners together. (Methods one and two are shown in the two photographs at right.)

Mounting needlepoint onto a support. If needlepoint is to be mounted onto any type of solid backing, its corners should be mitered and the edges pulled around the support. (Coasters on page 52 and clock face on page 72 were constructed in this manner.)

Spread a thin layer of white glue onto the back of the needlepoint; then position it directly onto a support cut the same size as the needlepointed section.

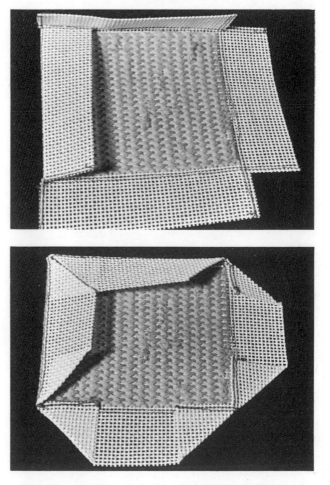

MITERING CORNERS, Method 1: fold edges to back of piece. Method 2: fold corners to form a diagonal edge; fold to back.

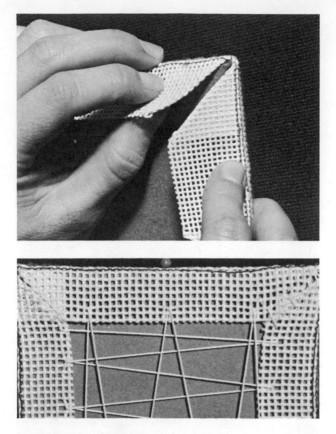

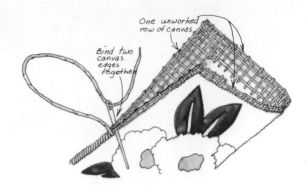

TWO CANVAS EDGES can be secured together. Work stitching through both canvases treating them as one.

PULL MITERED CORNERS around backing, then secure by gluing edges to back or by lacing opposite edges.

Draw the edges around, and glue them onto the back of the support (see the example above). If you prefer an alternate method of mounting, hold the edges snugly around the support by lacing carpet thread through opposite edges of the canvas (see photograph), rather than by gluing the edges. A piece of material or cardboard should be glued or stitched to the back of the piece to hide the lacing or glued edges.

Mounting a needlepoint piece onto a slip-seat chair is done in the same manner explained above. Simply pull the needlepoint over the seat and tack it into place. For a good fit, the needlepoint needs to be patterned after the shape of the seat. Several extra rows should be stitched to allow for the curve of the cushion as well as for the tuck-under. Tack the edges to the underside of the seat, taking tucks where necessary to keep needlepoint smooth on the face of the cushion.

Binding canvas edges together. Most needlepoint projects will fall into one of two categories: a single flat piece (mounted or unmounted); or two or more pieces that require binding two canvas edges together. Projects on pages 55, 64, or 70 demonstrate some of the items that have at least two edges of canvas joined.

A particularly good example of binding two canvas edges together is the eyeglass case. Most eyeglass cases are worked as a single piece, then folded and seamed together on at least two sides. To bind the edges, trim and fold back all the canvas edges so that there is at least one unstitched row of canvas (the process is the same as for edgings on page 44).

First seam the bottom of the eyeglass case (illustrated above), using the Gobelin stitch and stitching both edges of unworked canvas together. Then stitch up the side seam, again using a Gobelin stitch. Complete the case by working one of the stitches along its top edge.

Construct the lining slightly smaller than the finished needlepoint. Insert it by pushing it down into the case. Fold the top edge of the lining back, and slip stitch onto the inside of the case.

Edges can also be treated like any normal seam. With right sides together, stitch along the edge of the needlepointed section. Turn piece with right sides out.

By binding the canvas edges with the Gobelin stitch before you shape the item, a hand-sewn seam can be hidden between the last row of needlepoint and the single row of binding stitches.

SPECIAL FINISHING PROCESSES

Creativity comes to the foreground for the needlepointer not only in the first steps of design and color choices but also in the later step of finishing. Some craftsmen delight in discovering the most innovative ways of finishing their handwork. Of course, this invariably results in a certain degree of trial and error. But errors can often be rectified with some readjusting or "cheating" here and there.

The few specialized finishing processes that follow may help to suggest a way to complete your present needlepoint project. Hopefully, the suggestions may also stimulate you to develop new finishing methods of your own.

Boxed edges. Looking at the completed shape of a needlepointed box-edged pillow or three-dimensional needlepointed object, you might think that it defies all

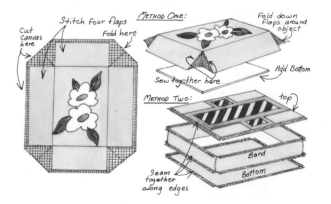

CONSTRUCTING A BOXED FORM is simple when you use either the "flap" method or three separate pieces.

TO MAKE A TASSEL, wind yarn on cardboard, secure, cut, bind top, then trim yarn ends and attach to needlepoint.

principles of working a needlepoint design as a flat plane. But by using an appropriate pattern, pieces are easily fitted together to form a top and sides. Either of two methods can be followed in creating three-dimensional forms: 1) the piece can be put together from three or more separate pieces (top, sides, and bottom) or 2) the three-dimensional square or rectangular needlepoint can be constructed from one flat piece with four flaps that fold down to form sides.

When constructing a boxed piece or three-dimensional item from three separate pieces, provide a top, a bottom, and a band for the side. The band should be long enough to fit around the circumference of the top and bottom piece (see illustration above); it can be as wide as you like.

When working with a boxed pillow covering, purchase foam or a pillow of the size you prefer. Then measure the depth and circumference of the proposed pillow from this. After you have completed the stitching join the three pieces, using one of the methods for joining canvases discussed on the previous page. Be sure to leave an edge open so that you can insert the pillow or support. (The band and bottom section do not necessarily have to be needlepointed; a complementary material can be substituted.)

A square or rectangular needlepointed item can be constructed from one piece patterned after the illustration above. Stitch four equal flaps beyond the completed main section that is to be the top of the object. Fold down the four flaps, tucking in the corners as illustrated above. Seam along the edges of each corner either by blind stitching or by a continental or Gobelin stitch. Insert whatever will be inside the casing (a piece of foam, a brick, or a block of wood), and sew or glue a bottom piece of cloth, cardboard, or wood into place (see illustration above). The door stop and paper weight (page 66 and page 67) were styled in this manner.

A final touch. One way to give a needlepointed piece its final creative touch is to add a tassel. Choose a yarn

color that goes well with your project. Wind the yarn around a piece of cardboard cut about the same length as the finished tassel will be. The more times you pull the yarn around the cardboard, the thicker the tassel.

Cut a length of yarn, slip it under looped yarn on one edge of the cardboard, and tie. Then cut through yarn at opposite end of cardboard as shown above in photograph 1. Remove cardboard.

Take another length of yarn (15 inches or more). Loop one end, placing the loop next to the tassel (see photograph 2). Beginning in the bottom of the upper third of the tassel, tightly wind the yarn around until you come to the single loop. Thread the yarn end that you were winding through the loop, and pull the other end of this loop until the loop and yarn end disappear under the wrapping (see photographs 3 and 4). Trim the uneven ends of the tassel.

Framing your needlepoint. Almost any frame can be used with needlepoint, but the frame's design should complement the pattern and colors of your finished piece. In order to be sure of a perfect fit, purchase the frame before you begin to stitch.

After the needlepoint is blocked, mount it onto masonite or a thin piece of board, as explained on page 46. Then slip it into the frame. The needlepoint picture can be held into the frame by another piece of wood or by small nails perpendicularly tacked into the inside edge of the frame's back.

Needlepoint Projects
for Everyone

Projects with graphed designs

Ideas for future projects

Self-Designing Bell Pull

This bell pull is a good project for the beginner who wants to practice the techniques of the continental and basketweave stitch without being concerned with creating a design. Using regular worsted variegated knitting yarn and these basic stitches, you can automatically create a simple striped pattern.

MATERIALS:

No. 10 canvas, tapestry needle (no. 18), one skein of variegated yarn, felt for backing, three bells, short dowel with knobs for ends.

DIRECTIONS:

1. Bind a piece of canvas about 7 inches wide and 20 inches long.
2. Using an indelible marker, outline the border of your bell pull in the center of the canvas. Copy the pattern shown on the right (the piece measures approximately 3 inches by 16 inches to the point). The pull is divided vertically into three equal areas, each ten stitches wide.
3. Starting at top right corner of the center area, stitch the center portion in basketweave (ten stitches wide). To achieve the striped pattern, cut the lengths of yarn directly from the skein as you need them. Always thread the yarn so that the tail is the same color as your last stitch.
4. After completing the center portion, begin the two side panels using the continental stitch. Cut your lengths of yarn in the same manner as before. Stitch the first row in the right panel, then continue this row directly into the left panel by weaving the thread through the back of the basketweave section. (Remember, when working the continental stitch, after each row turn entire piece upside down to begin next row.)
5. Once you have completed the stitching, make sure all the ends are tied off and clipped. Block the piece as explained on page 42. Worsted knitting yarn will be more difficult to block than your regular needlepoint wools. You may need to block the piece several times.
6. Machine stitch around needlepointed section. Cut off all but 1 inch of unworked canvas around the stitched portion. Fold canvas edges under and whip stitch to the back of the piece, mitering corners where needed (see page 45).
7. Cut a piece of felt in a contrasting color about ⅛ inch larger than the sides and point of your stitched canvas. Cut the top portion of the felt long enough to be looped over a wooden dowel (approximately 8 inches from the top of the needlepoint). Blind stitch the

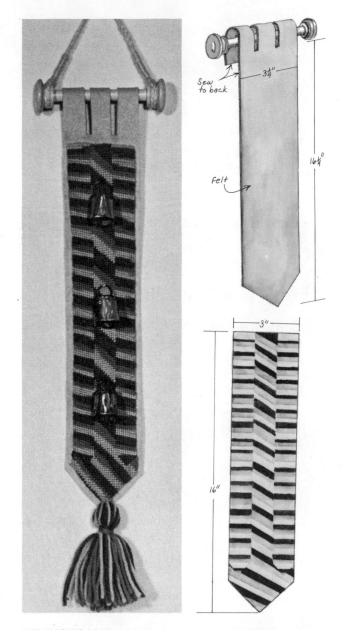

USE VARIEGATED YARN to create striped needlepoint pattern. Attach needlepoint to felt and loop straps over dowel.

needlepoint to the felt. Cut two vertical slots ½ inch wide and 7⅞ inches deep from the top of the felt. Fold the straps over the dowel and sew them to the back of the bell pull.

8. Secure the three bells with variegated yarn stitching over the bell handle and through both thicknesses of needlepoint and felt.
9. Make the bottom tassel as illustrated on page 47, then sew it onto the tip of the bell pull.

Anyone for Chess or Checkers?

(Color photograph on inside front cover)

Making your own chessboard or checkerboard gives you a chance to break away from the traditional black and red color scheme and to choose a color combination that matches the decor of your home. The chessboard is needlepointed entirely in the continental and basketweave stitch. When it is finished, mount the chessboard on a light board and cover with a protective square of glass. Placed on top of a small low table, it becomes a functional piece of furniture as well as a game.

MATERIALS:

No. 10 mono canvas, tapestry needle (no. 18), three-strand Persian yarn (suggested colors: deep olive green and a lighter olive green), wood or heavy cardboard for backing, small table and protective glass 15 inches square (optional).

DIRECTIONS:

1. Bind a piece of no. 10 mono canvas about 18 inches by 18 inches.
2. Using an indelible marker, outline the border of the chessboard in the center of the canvas (15 inches square). Measure 1½ inches in from this border and draw another square in the center of the larger one (13½ inches).
3. Transfer the pattern of the chessboard onto the canvas or follow the pattern shown at right.
4. Starting at the top right corner of the inner square, stitch the first of the 64 squares. Continue stitching from the upper right corner down to the lower left corner of the canvas alternating the squares in light and dark yarn colors.
5. Stitch the border design following the pattern shown at right.
6. Block the chessboard as explained on page 42. Since the design is completely geometric, the vertical and horizontal lines are extremely important to the overall appearance of your piece.
7. Machine stitch canvas around the edge of the needlepointed section.
8. Trim the canvas edges to within 1 inch of the design and miter all four corners as explained in method 2, page 45.
9. Spread a thin layer of white glue on the wrong side of the needlepoint. Slip a piece of wood or cardboard (15 inches square) onto the back of the needlepoint. Draw mitered corners around the support and secure the edges of the canvas to the back as explained on page 46. Attach a 15-inch square of felt as backing.

KATHRYN ARTHURS

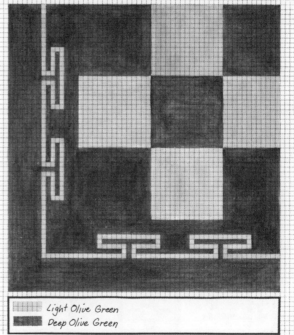

Light Olive Green
Deep Olive Green

REPEAT SQUARES AND BORDER DESIGN until you stitch sixty-four squares. (Also see inside front cover.)

10. You may like to add an edging to hide where the canvas folds over the board (see page 44).
11. The board can be left as it is at this point, or you can place the mounted canvas on a small table and position a 15-inch square of glass on top of it.

Elegant Glass Coasters
(Color photograph on inside front cover)

Needlepointed glass coasters are fast little projects that any host or hostess would be flattered to receive. Use a good colorfast wool that can be sponged easily if the coasters become soiled. If you want to spray the coasters with a protective coating, test the yarn and any ink or paint you plan to use to make certain the chemicals in the spray do not cause the colors to run or blur.

Four patterns are shown below: the two on the left are a pair and the two on the right were designed to go together. You can vary the design of each coaster by transposing color areas.

ALYSON S. GONSALVES

AFRICAN AND PRIMITIVE textile designs were used as ideas for coaster patterns. (Also see inside front cover.)

MATERIALS:

No. 12 canvas, tapestry needle (no. 18 or no. 19), two-strand Persian yarn (suggested colors for design one: black, brown, off-white, orange, yellow; suggested for design two: purple, green, off-white; suggested colors for design three: plum, dark green, light green, beige, cream, brown, gold; suggested colors for design four: plum, yellow, off-white, black, light green), felt for backing, large flat-sided plastic bottle.

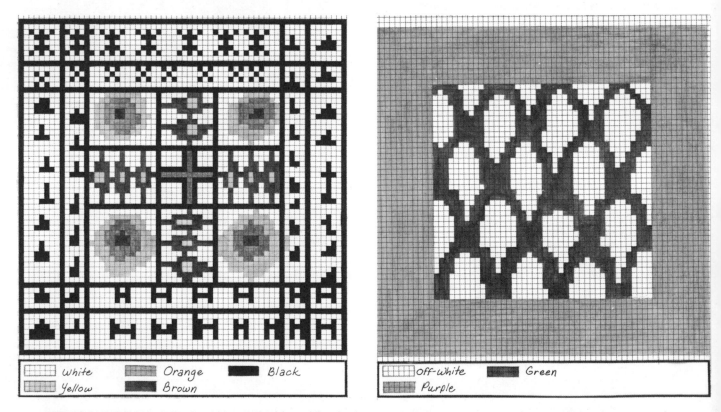

	White		Orange		Black
	Yellow		Brown		

	Off-White		Green
	Purple		

DETAILS AND SINGLE LINES should be stitched first; fill in background last. To size pattern for direct tracing, enlarge 30%, then trace it onto your canvas using an indelible marker. To vary design, use different colors.

DIRECTIONS:

1. Bind a piece of no. 12 canvas approximately 6½ inches by 6½ inches for one coaster.

2. Using an indelible marker, outline the border of one coaster in the center of the canvas (4½ inches by 4½ inches).

3. Transfer one of the designs onto the canvas or begin stitching using the graphs below.

4. First stitch all lines and detail, then fill in the larger background areas. Use basketweave where possible.

5. When completed, block the coaster as explained on page 42, or cover with a cloth and steam with an iron if little distortion occurred.

6. Machine stitch around the needlepointed section, then trim canvas edge to within ½ inch of the stitched portion. Prepare to miter the corners as explained on page 45, method 2.

7. From a flat-sided plastic bottle, cut some 4½-inch squares. These will be used as a stiff backing.

8. Spread a thin layer of white glue on the back side of the needlepoint then position the plastic square on the back. Pull the mitered corners around the plastic, then glue or lace the edges as explained on page 46.

9. Cut a felt square for the backing and sew it onto the back of the coaster along edges of the needlepoint.

10. Crochet a single chain of complementary colored yarn and sew it along the four edges of the coaster.

ALYSON S. GONSALVES

INSECTS AND FRUIT are good themes for kitchen or food related needlepoint pieces. (See inside front cover.)

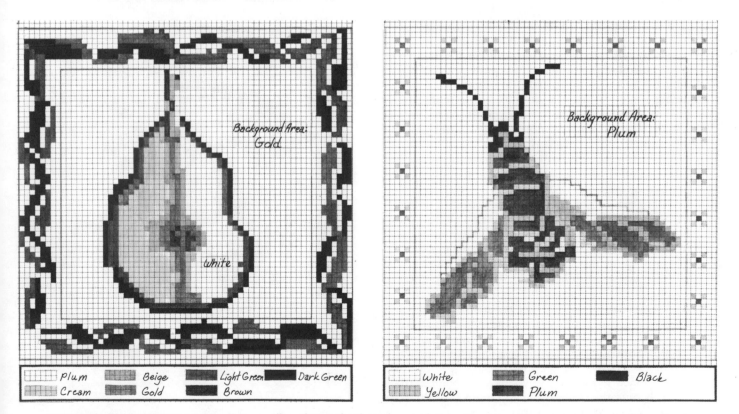

Background Area: Gold

White

	Plum		Beige		Light Green		Dark Green
	Cream		Gold		Brown		

Background Area: Plum

	White		Green		Black
	Yellow		Plum		

PEAR AND BEE PATTERNS work well for a pillow design if enlarged several sizes. To size pattern as a coaster and for direct tracing, enlarge 30% then trace it onto your canvas, using an indelible marker.

Pocket Chic

(Color photographs on inside front and back cover)

Two designs are shown here for simple and decorative pockets that can be made singly or in matched pairs. The design on the right was inspired from the primitive, yet uniquely sophisticated, appliqué work of the San Blas Indians. Adapted from Pennsylvania Dutch folk art, the second pocket also has a refreshing simplicity. The pockets can be attached to jackets, pants, dresses, or any clothing; but if the article of clothing is washable, you may want to put snaps on the back of the pocket for easy removal. Choose yarn colors coordinated with your outfit, and make the pocket a size that is comfortable and attractive on you. The basketweave was used extensively in the two designs; however, a decorative stitch can be used for the background if it covers the canvas well.

MATERIALS:

No. 14 canvas, tapestry needle (no. 20), two-strand Persian yarn (suggested colors for design one: crimson, gold, black; suggested colors for design two: yellow, blue, green, red, white), lining material.

DIRECTIONS:

1. For pocket one or two, cut and bind a piece of canvas approximately 9 inches by 9 inches.
2. Using an indelible marker, outline the border of your pocket in the center of the canvas (pocket one is about 4½ inches wide and 5½ inches deep. Pocket two is about 5½ inches wide and 6 inches to the point).
3. Trace the design onto your canvas or follow the graphs. Stitch the center portion of your design using the basketweave as much as possible.
4. Fill in the background area with basketweave or any other stitch choosing from the decorative stitches described on pages 22-35.
5. Block the pocket as explained on page 42, or lightly steam iron it if little distortion occurred.
6. Machine stitch around the needlepointed section, then trim the canvas to within 1 inch of the stitched portion. Miter the corners as explained on page 45. Turn under and whip stitch the canvas edges to the wrong side of the pocket.
7. Using your finished pocket as a pattern, cut a piece of closely woven cloth ½ inch larger than the pocket.
8. Place wrong sides of lining and needlepoint together. Turn under cut edges of lining and blind stitch to the back of the needlepoint.
9. To attach the pocket to your outfit, blind stitch it directly onto the clothing. Or add snaps near the edge of the lined side of the pocket and sew snaps to clothing in corresponding spaces.

Continued on next page.

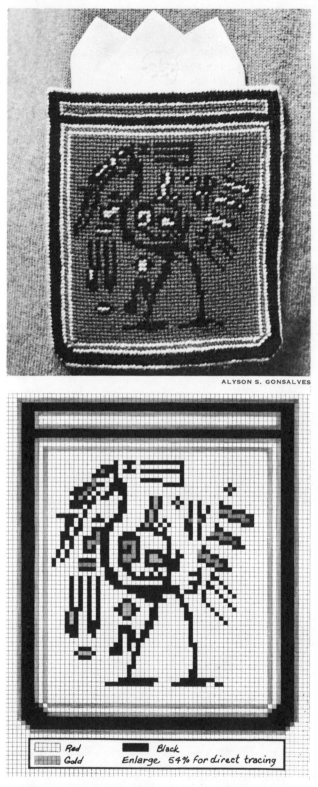

ALYSON S. GONSALVES

	Red		Black
	Gold		Enlarge 54% for direct tracing

IMAGE OF CRANE was stitched in continental; the background was done in basketweave. (See inside front cover.)

USE PRIMARY COLORS to accentuate the simplicity of a bold pattern. (Also see inside front cover.)

| | Cream | | Green | | Blue |
| | Yellow | | Red | | |

TRACE PATTERN DIRECTLY by enlarging it 70%. Begin with center motif, then fill in background.

Shear Beauty

Every needleworker needs a pair of small scissors, and a case for them is the greatest protection from loss or damage. The needlepointed scissors case can be a simple abstract design (see example, right). This design developed as the stitching progressed, and because odd bits of yarn from previous needlepoint projects were used, the color scheme also developed with very little planning.

The shape of the case was patterned after the paper case that protected the scissors when they were purchased. Finishing requires one major seam and a binding stitch along the top. The case can be lined or left unlined.

MATERIALS:

No. 10/20 Penelope canvas (the piece was worked in petit point), tapestry needle (no. 21 or no. 22), one-strand Persian yarn (suggested colors: black, forest
Continued on next page.

CONE-SHAPED SCISSORS CASE is worked in petit point. Abstract design can lead to many other innovative patterns.

Continued from previous page.

green, green, yellow, pale green), small snap for fastening, felt for lining material (optional).

DIRECTIONS:

1. Bind a piece of no. 10 Penelope canvas 9 inches by 8½ inches. Using an indelible marker, outline the shape of the case as shown below.
2. Separate the paired threads to prepare for the petit point work.
3. Transfer the design onto the canvas or begin stitching following the graph below.
4. Once the piece is completed, block or press it slightly with an iron as explained on page 42.
5. Machine stitch around needlepointed section, then trim canvas edges to within ½ inch of the stitched portion.
6. Fold over the top edge of the case, leaving one unworked row of the canvas above the needlepointed section. Work a row of Gobelin stitches using two strands to cover the canvas well (see page 29).
7. Fold under the edges on the remaining three sides and stitch to the back.

8. Cut a piece of felt the dimensions and shape of the unfolded case. Blind stitch lining onto the wrong side of the needlepoint. Position a snap near top edge so that once the case is folded, it can be snapped closed.
9. Fold the case into a cone shape, then using clear nylon thread, stitch the two long edges together (see illustration below). Stitch the bottom point closed. To flatten the case, gently press with the iron (have the seam running on the backside of the case).

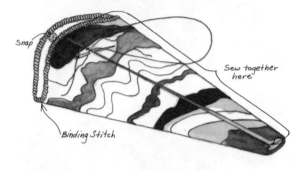

HAND STITCH two long edges together with clear nylon thread. Add snap to opposite sides of top inside edge.

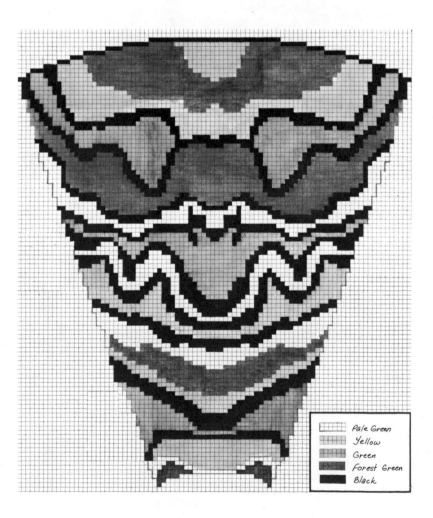

USE THE GRAPH as a general guide but experiment as much as you would like, adding colors and lines wherever it is convenient.

▦	Pale Green
▦	Yellow
▦	Green
▦	Forest Green
■	Black

A Belt Maori Style

(Color photograph on inside front cover)

The Maoris of New Zealand inspired the geometric, bead-like design of the belt shown here. The vivid colors and bold pattern reflect the personality of this brave, vigorous, and athletic tribe. The belt is simple to reproduce because it is a repetitive geometric pattern. Mounted on a stiff buckram lining, the belt holds its shape well. Fasten it securely around the waist with several leather thongs.

ALYSON S. GONSALVES

MODERN ADAPTATION of Maori belt design is simple geometric repeat pattern. (See inside front cover.)

MATERIALS:

No. 10 mono canvas, tapestry needle (no 18), tapestry wool (suggested colors: crimson, black, off-white, yellow-gold), 3-inch buckram, 4 leather thongs (approximately 4 yards), grommet tool and grommets.

DIRECTIONS:

1. Bind a piece of canvas 9 inches wide and the length of your waist measurement plus 6 inches.
2. Using an indelible marker, outline the border of the belt in the center of the canvas three inches wide by the measurement of your waist (you can measure your waist so that there would be a slight opening in the front between the two ends of the belt; see the photograph above).
3. Mark the center back of the belt. The main design should be centered here so that at each end the design will be the same.
4. Using an indelible marker, either trace the repeat design onto the canvas or follow the graph shown below. Since it is a geometric repeat pattern, you may prefer following the graph.

5. Stitch the single dark lines first, then fill in the larger areas using basketweave as much as possible.
6. After the stitching is completed, block the belt as explained on page 42.
7. Machine stitch around the needlepointed section.
8. Trim canvas edge to within 1 inch of the stitched section. Cut and miter corners as explained in method 1, page 45. Fold the edges so that one unworked row of canvas is left, and work the Gobelin stitch around all four edges.
10. Hand stitch buckram to back of belt, folding under the cut ends.
11. Following the directions that accompany the grommet kit, carefully position the grommet tool through the needlepoint so that the canvas threads will not be cut. Punch two evenly spaced holes at each end.
12. Thread leather thongs through grommet as illustrated below. Each thong should be approximately 36 inches long or 18 inches when doubled over.

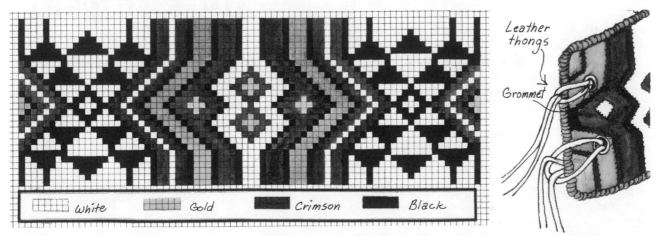

| White | Gold | Crimson | Black |

COUNT OFF STITCHES following graph above to make accurate geometric pattern or transfer design directly by enlarging 70%, then tracing it onto the canvas. When the belt is completed, loop leather thongs through grommets as illustrated above.

His·and·Her Watchbands

Wrist watches have become more than just a practical item to wear. With interchangeable bands the watch is transformed into a versatile piece of jewelry appropriate for any style dress. A needlepointed band is durable, a unique method of using your canvas work, and the project is simple and takes little time to complete. Choose from the two designs here: one was designed for a woman and the other for a man.

MATERIALS:

No. 14 canvas, tapestry needle (no. 20), two-strand Persian yarn (suggested colors for woman's watch band: off-white, orange, light green; suggested colors for man's watchband: off-white, tomato red, olive green), small (no. 0000) snaps or large flat skirt hooks, grosgrain ribbon for backing.

DIRECTIONS:

1. Measure around your wrist leaving an opening for the watch face. Bind a piece of canvas about 3¾ inches wide and 2 inches longer than the measurement around your wrist.
2. Using an indelible marker, outline the border of your watchband in the center of the canvas (¾ inch wide by whatever length you need).
3. Trace the design onto your canvas or follow one of the graphs at right.
4. Stitch in the design using the basketweave as much as possible.
5. Block the watchband as explained on page 42 or steam iron if it is just slightly misshapen.
6. Stitch around needlepointed section, then trim canvas to within ¼ inch of the stitched section. Fold over the canvas edges, mitering corners as explained in method 1, page 45. (If you use white glue to secure the canvas edge to the back of the band, it will dry in the position you leave it.)
7. Measure a length of ¾-inch grosgrain ribbon (at least 3½ inches longer than the length of the finished needlepoint). Stitch the ribbon to the back of the needlepoint leaving at least 1¾ inches beyond both ends of the band.
8. If you would like a removable watchband, stitch snaps on both ends of the grosgrain ribbon. Be sure that the snaps are small enough to slip between the bar and watch face (see illustration at right).
9. If you would like a permanent watchband, pull one end of the grosgrain ribbon through the bar at the edge of the clock face and stitch it to the back of the watch band. Sew a skirt hook to the other end of the gros grain ribbon as illustrated.

ALYSON S. GONSALVES

SIMPLE PATTERNS can be worked in an hour if you make a small needlepoint item, such as a watchband.

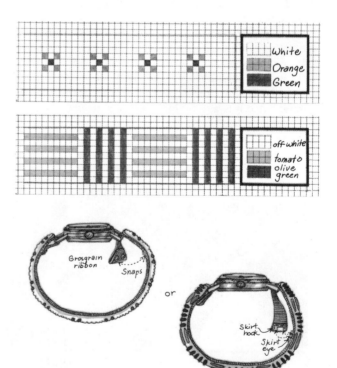

White
Orange
Green

off-white
tomato
olive green

STITCH IN ENTIRE DESIGN, then finish by sewing needlepoint to ribbon and adding snaps for easy removal.

Needlepoint Covered Buttons

Needlepoint buttons are an exquisite way to finish off a jacket or newly knitted sweater. The buttons can echo the pattern of the garment or be the focal point of an entire outfit.

The bold and simple examples shown below are designed as primitive interpretations of birds and fish.

MATERIALS:

No. 14 canvas for large buttons, petit point canvas or embroidery cloth for any button smaller than 1½ inches, tapestry needle (size depends on canvas), one or two-strand Persian yarn (suggested colors for button one: blue, yellow, orange; suggested colors for button two: cream, green, black), button kit (do not try to cover any button less than ¾ inch), backing material.

DIRECTIONS:

(Note: the two buttons below were done on no. 14 canvas. Because of the bulkiness of the needlepoint, the section of the button kit that normally is clamped into the back to hold the material in position must be replaced by cardboard and stuffing. The process is ex-

plained in step 7. If you use a smaller mesh canvas, you should be able to easily fit in the back portion of the button kit.)

1. Bind a piece of no. 14 canvas approximately 3½ inches by 3½ inches.

2. Using an indelible marker, outline the border of the button (use the pattern illustrated on the button kit). You will have to stitch several rows beyond this border to allow for the curvature of the button and the bulkiness of the needlepoint.

3. Stitch entire area with suggested design.

4. Once the button is completed, machine stitch canvas around the edge of the needlepoint.

5. Moisten entire piece, then pull over button form.

6. Carefully trim canvas until it is approximately ⅛ inch to ¼ inch from stitching.

7. If button back cannot be clamped into place as explained on the button kit, cut a thin piece of cardboard to fit snugly into the back of the button. Pad with a small piece of cotton or material, then cover back with a closely woven cloth such as felt (see illustration below). (Cut hole in cloth and cardboard for button hook.) Hand sew felt around edge of needlepoint.

8. Attach button to clothing but remove when outfit is cleaned.

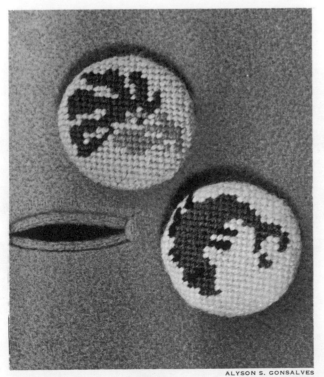

ALYSON S. GONSALVES

FOCAL POINT of an entire outfit, these buttons are simple but sophisticated animal designs.

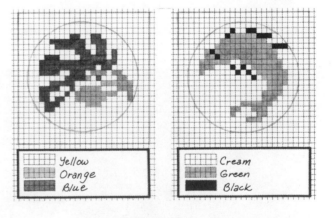

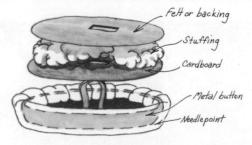

SMALL DESIGNS are easier to follow from a graph. Construct button as directed on kit or as shown above.

Tray or Placemat Wall Holder

(Color photograph on inside front cover)

Your trays or placemats can be stored not only conveniently but also attractively if they hang from a lovely needlepointed tray holder. This holder, complete with a decorative tray, could be a unique and greatly appreciated gift for a bride.

The design for the tray holder could match your china pattern or the curtains and wall paper of the room you intend to hang it in. The pop-art design of the example at right will blend into most any modern day decor.

MATERIALS:

No. 12 canvas, tapestry needle (no. 18 or no. 19), two or three-strand Persian wool (suggested colors: deep purple, navy blue, magenta, violet, hot pink, and yellow-gold), two-inch grosgrain ribbon (38 inches for each strap), wooden drapery ring.

DIRECTIONS:

1. Cut and bind two pieces of canvas, each 6 inches wide by 22 inches long. Using an indelible marker, outline the border of the straps (2 inches wide by 18 inches long) in the center of the canvas.

2. Trace the design onto your canvas or follow the graph shown below. Stitch center motif before filling in the background. A decorative stitch could be substituted for the basketweave background.

3. Block the straps as described on page 42.

4. Machine stitch around the needlepointed section, then trim the unstitched canvas edges to within 1 inch of the needlepoint. Turn canvas edges under, leaving one unworked row of canvas beyond the needlepointed section. Using a complementary colored yarn (three strands), stitch the upright Gobelin stitch along all four edges of each strap.

5. Cut the grosgrain ribbon into two strips, each 38 inches long. Sew half of one length onto the back of the needlepoint as lining. Loop the remaining half of the ribbon through the drapery ring and stitch the ribbon end to the top of the needlepoint (see illustration opposite page). Repeat the same process for the second strap.

6. Pull one strap over on top of the other strap, then to hold them in position, stitch a row just beneath the ring, as shown on opposite page.

7. To secure the straps in this angled position, sew a length of grosgrain ribbon from one strap to the other about mid-way on the back of the grosgrain ribbon as illustrated on opposite page.

FREE-FORM IN DESIGN, these straps can be a springboard for other design ideas. Enlarge graph 25% if you prefer to trace the design directly onto the canvas. Stitch from the short side down to the bottom short side.

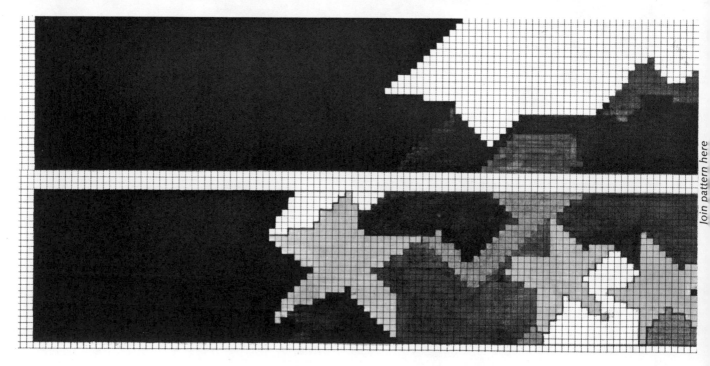

Join pattern here

CAROL H. GOFORTH

PLACEMATS OR TRAYS become part of wall decor when hung in needlepointed straps. (See inside front cover.)

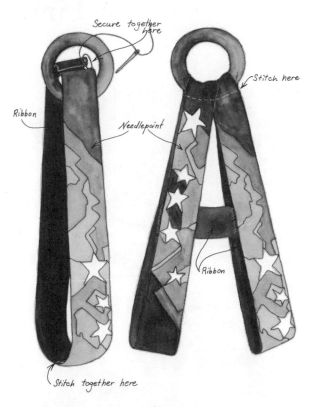

ATTACH RIBBON to back and end of needlepoint, then secure on ring. Add horizontal ribbon to hold straps in place.

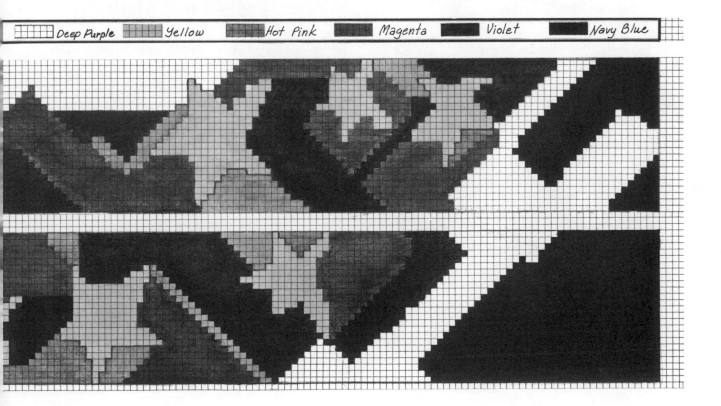

A Pin's Best Friend

(Color photograph on inside back cover)

LILLIAN JANE FEIGHT DEL CARLO

White	Chartreuse	Green		Black (pupil of eye).
Off-White	Turquoise	Blue		

ENLARGE FISH DESIGN about 110% to use for direct tracing onto the canvas. (See inside back cover.)

Pincushions are a popular needlepoint project because they are small, quick to make, and a good gift to send to anyone who does needlework. Four examples are shown: two are finished in the same manner as a knife-edged pillow, and two are attractively bound in wooden napkin rings.

MATERIALS:

No. 10 mono canvas for the fish and butterfly design, no. 12 mono canvas for the oblong shaped piece, no. 10/20 Penelope canvas for the elephant pincushion (worked in petit point), tapestry needle (size depends on canvas used), Persian or tapestry yarn in a size corresponding to the canvas (suggested colors: fish—black, white, chartreuse, turquoise, blue, green, off-white; butterfly—black, orange, yellow orange, purple, green, rust; oblong shape—four shades of green; elephant—red, light blue, pink, chartreuse, white), felt for backing, wooden napkin rings, styrofoam, kapok, dacron, or foam rubber for stuffing.

DIRECTIONS (fish and butterfly pincushion):

1. For the fish, bind a piece of canvas 9 inches by 7½ inches. Bind a piece of canvas 8½ inches by 8¼ inches for the butterfly pincushion.
2. Using an indelible marker, outline the border of the fish pincushion (5 inches by 3½ inches) or the border

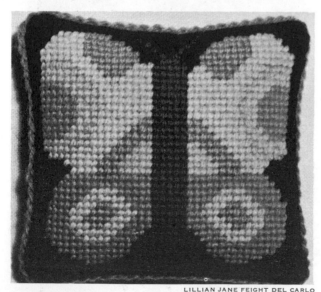

LILLIAN JANE FEIGHT DEL CARLO

RAINBOW OF COLORS can be used in a butterfly motif. Background is Scottish stitch. (See inside back cover.)

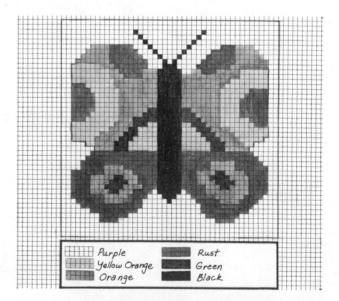

Purple		Rust	
Yellow Orange		Green	
Orange		Black	

BUTTERFLY is in basketweave; area of 3 squares on chart equals Scottish stitch in background. To trace, enlarge 90%.

of the butterfly pincushion (4¼ inches by 4¼ inches).

3. Transfer the designs shown on left page onto the canvas or begin stitching the center design following the pattern from the graph. Stitch the fish or butterfly entirely in basketweave.

4. After the center design is completed, stitch the background in the Scottish stitch (explained on page 23).

5. Block the piece and finish in the same manner as the knife-edged pillow, pages 43-44 (eliminate the inner pillow — just stuff the needlepoint casing directly).

6. Crochet a single chain in a complementary colored yarn and sew it to the edge of the cushion.

DIRECTIONS (napkin ring pincushions):

(The size of the two napkin ring pincushions are determined entirely by the size of the napkin ring you are able to purchase.)

1. To begin the oblong-shaped pincushion, bind a piece of canvas approximately 6½ inches long by 3 inches wide. Mark off the area to be worked the same as the hole in the napkin ring.

2. Work approximately 17 rows of Gobelin stitch, arranging the colors from light to dark. Also vary the depth of each row by stitching over a different number of meshes each time (see chart below).
Continued on next page.

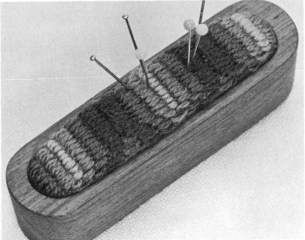

LILLIAN JANE FEIGHT DEL CARLO

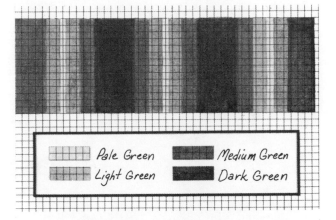

Pale Green — Medium Green
Light Green — Dark Green

LENGTH OF GOBELIN STITCH changes each row. Treat graph as representation of canvas. Position colors from dark to light.

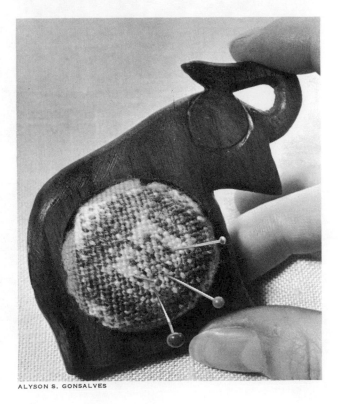

ALYSON S. GONSALVES

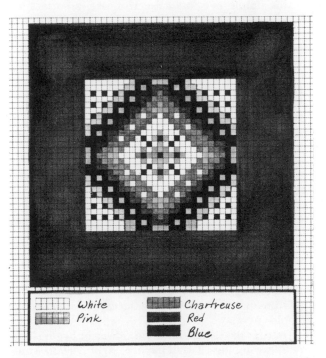

White — Chartreuse
Pink — Red
Blue

PETIT POINT DESIGN is easiest when worked from graph rather than tracing design to canvas. (See inside back cover.)

Continued from previous page.

3. Cut a piece of styrofoam slightly deeper than the napkin ring but the same circumference as the hole.
4. Pull the needlepoint over the styrofoam, then push them both into the napkin ring hole as shown below.
5. Trim off any excess canvas and glue canvas edges to the underside of the styrofoam. Cut pieces of card-

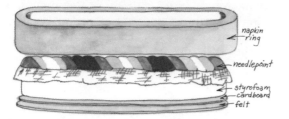

SECURE NEEDLEPOINT around the styrofoam, then push it up through the hole of the napkin ring.

board and felt the size of the bottom of the napkin ring and glue into place.

1. To begin the elephant-shaped pincushion, bind a piece of Penelope (10/20) canvas 4 inches square.
2. With an indelible marker, mark off a square in the center of the canvas about 1½ inches by 1½ inches.
3. Carefully separate the canvas threads within the marked square making the canvas 20, rather than 10, stitches to the inch.
4. Following the graphed pattern on previous page, stitch in the geometric design.
5. Cut a piece of styrofoam (half of a ball) and, holding the finished needlepoint around the styrofoam, push it into the napkin ring as shown at left.
6. Cut off any excess canvas, then glue edges to the bottom of the styrofoam. Cut a piece of cardboard and felt the size of the bottom of the napkin ring. Glue them into place.

A Case in Point

In needlepoint, you can simulate on canvas the lovely fur patterns of such rare animals as the zebra depicted on this simple eyeglass case. The case, a perfect gift for a man or woman, is easily made from a single needlepointed piece that is folded and seamed along the side.

MATERIALS:

No. 14 mono canvas, tapestry needle (no. 20), two-strand Persian yarn or tapestry wool (suggested colors: off-white, charcoal brown), lining material.

DIRECTIONS:

1. Bind a piece of No. 14 mono canvas, 10½ inches by 10¾ inches.
2. Using an indelible marker, draw the outline of the case 6½ inches wide by 6¾ inches deep. Indicate where the piece will fold in the center (3¼ inches in from the edge). Check the size with the glasses you will store in the case to be sure the case is large enough to hold them.
3. Transfer the design onto the canvas or begin stitching following the charted pattern, right. (If you would like to stitch in your initials, refer to page 76 for suggested alphabets.)

Continued on next page.

LILLIAN JANE FEIGHT DEL CARLO

ZEBRA DESIGN is bold abstraction. Two colors with simple stitching creates a smashing presentation.

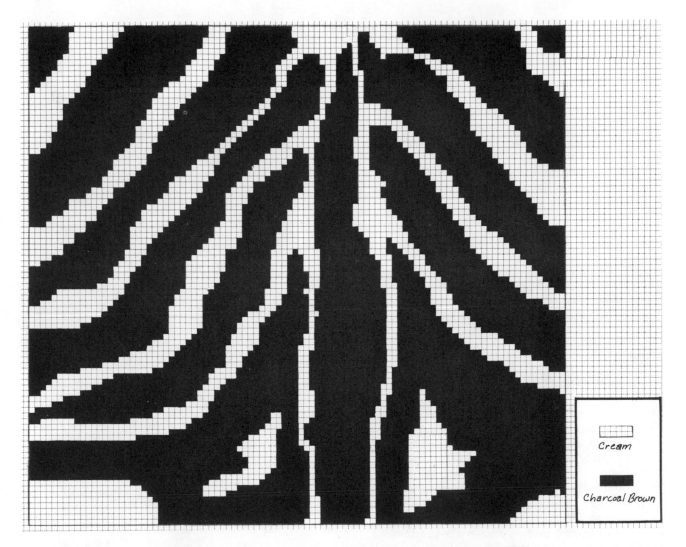

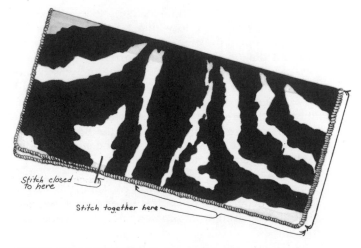

Cream

Charcoal Brown

EASY TO FOLLOW, the graph can be used or a tracing can be made from the chart if it is enlarged 27%. If you would like to add your initials to the design, see box on page 76 for some suggested alphabets.

4. When the piece is completed, block or lightly press the case with the iron as explained on page 42.

5. Machine stitch around the needlepointed section and cut all the corners for mitering. Trim the canvas edges to within ¾ inch from the stitched section. Fold under the edges and miter the corners as explained on page 45. Lightly iron or stitch the edges to the back of the needlepoint.

6. Cut a piece of felt material the same size as the case, and blind stitch the felt to the back of the needle-pointed section.

7. Fold the case in half. Using clear nylon thread, stitch the side and bottom closed (see illustration). Along the side, leave approximately 2 inches from the top unseamed (see illustration).

8. Crochet a single chain in a matching color of yarn. It should be long enough to go along the top, down the side seam, and along the bottom edges.

Stitch closed to here

Stitch together here

STITCH SIDES TOGETHER starting a little below top of case. Crochet single chain, then secure as edging.

Decorative Doorstop

Working needlepoint over a three-dimensional form is a great challenge to needleworkers. The actual construction of the piece is not as difficult as deciding on a design that is appealing from every possible viewpoint. One of the easiest solutions is to use an overall repeat pattern, as shown on this needlepointed doorstop. The base for the doorstop is an ordinary brick, but once concealed in the lovely needlepointed casing, it can prop open even the most elegant of doors.

MATERIALS:

No. 12 mono canvas, tapestry needle (no. 18 or no. 19), two or three-strand Persian wool or tapestry wool (suggested colors: cream, cocoa brown, rust, gold), felt for the bottom, building brick.

DIRECTIONS:

1. Measure the brick you plan to use (the common dimensions for a building brick are 8 to 8½ inches in length, 3¾ to 3⅞ inches in width, and 2¼ to 2½ inches in depth). With these dimensions in mind, measure, cut, and bind the edges of a piece of canvas approximately 19 inches by 15 inches.
2. Using an indelible marker, outline the border of the casing in the center of the canvas using the pattern shown at right and discussed on page 47. Add ¼ inch to each edge to allow for any shrinkage. (The dimensions for the casing are based on an average-sized brick.)
3. Transfer the leopard pattern onto the canvas or begin stitching using the charted design on opposite page. (Chart shown is only a portion of overall design.)
4. Once completed, block the casing as explained on page 42.
5. Machine stitch around needlepointed section, then trim the canvas edge to within 1 inch of the needlepoint, except at the corners. Don't cut out the corners, but cut diagonally across the corner; see at right.
6. Fold the casing over the brick and stitch the corner edges together with a needle and clear nylon thread.
7. Fold under the bottom edges of canvas and glue them to the brick, or lace them as explained on page 46. Cut a piece of felt the size of the bottom of the brick. Glue the felt into place or blind stitch it to the bottom edge of the needlepoint.
Note: Before the needlepointed casing is pulled around the brick, a slip cover of muslin or felt can be glued directly to the brick. This helps prevent the needlepointed casing from slipping once it is secured into place.

Continued on next page.

GINNY CAMPBELL

FUR PATTERNS of wild animals such as the leopard are often excellent sources of repeat designs for needlepoint.

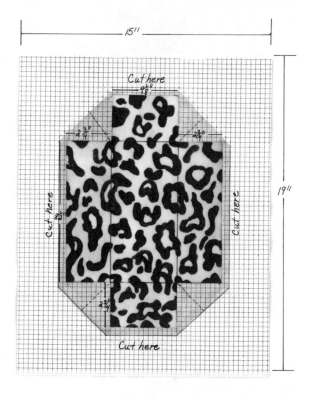

USE PATTERN above to construct boxed casing for brick. Fold on dotted line and cut along gray section.

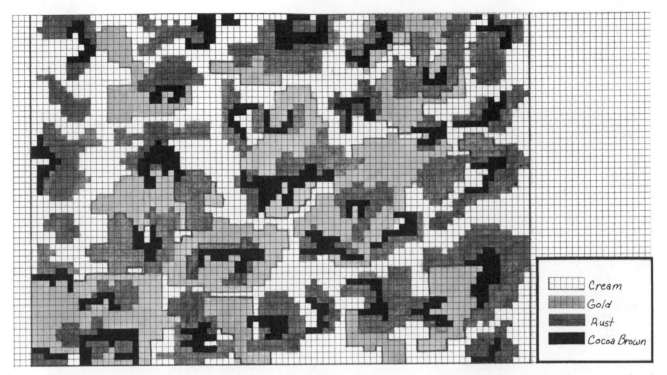

	Cream
	Gold
	Rust
	Cocoa Brown

USE CHART to create overall repeat leopard pattern. Keep the colors simple or true to life. See page 78 for clever example of another door stop that uses the shape of the brick as part of the design.

Scottish Stitch Paperweight

A wood block covered with a needlepointed casing and constructed in the same manner as the brick doorstop gives you a decorative as well as a functional paperweight. The example shown here was worked entirely in the Scottish stitch and in several shades of green. The gradation of yarn colors from dark to light in diagonal rows helps to conceal the seams along each corner. A good gift idea for the student or office worker, this project is fast and can lead to endless variations.

MATERIALS:

No. 14 mono canvas, tapestry needle (no. 20), two or three-strand Persian yarn or tapestry wool (suggested colors: four shades of green), a 3½-inch wood block cut from a finished 4x4, felt for bottom.

DIRECTIONS:

1. Bind a piece of No. 14 mono canvas approximately 17½ inches square.
2. Using an indelible marker, outline the border of the
Continued on next page.

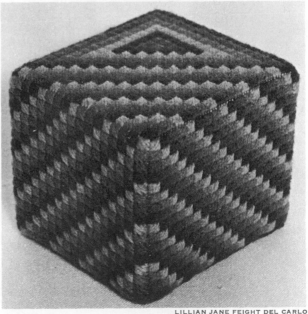

LILLIAN JANE FEIGHT DEL CARLO

PAPERWEIGHT is constructed like the doorstop but is done in Scottish stitch and covers a wood block.

Continued from previous page.

casing in the center of the canvas (use the pattern and dimensions shown at right).

3. Following the graph below, begin stitching the Scottish stitch (see page 23). Remember that each complete stitch will cover a square area of three meshes by three meshes. Use the graph below on the left for the four sides of the block. Use the graph below on the right for the top of the block. (Try to match the diagonal rows along the corners.)

4. Stitch one extra row of Scottish stitches along each edge for ease. (The dimensions given allow for this extra row.)

5. After stitching is completed, block the casing as explained on page 42.

6. Machine stitch around the needlepointed section, then trim the canvas edge to within 1 inch of the needlepoint except at the corners where you make a diagonal cut as illustrated at right.

7. Fold the casing over the wood block and stitch the corner edges together with clear nylon thread.

8. Fold under the bottom edges of canvas and glue them to the block or lace them as explained on page 46. Cut a piece of felt the size of the bottom of the block. Glue the felt into place or blind stitch it to the bottom edges of the needlepoint.

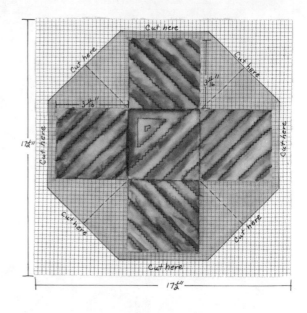

CENTER SHAPE of casing on canvas. Once completed, fold on dotted lines; cut along gray section.

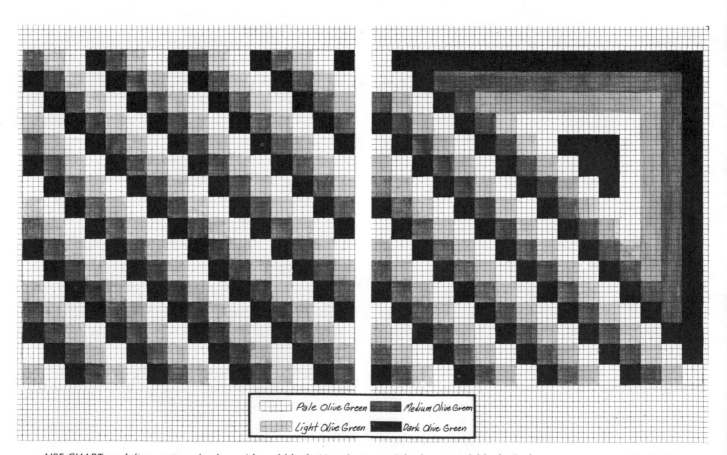

USE CHART on left as pattern for four sides of block. Use chart on right for top of block. Each gray square represents one Scottish stitch that covers a square area of 3 meshes by 3 meshes. Work colors from dark to light.

Pale Olive Green   Medium Olive Green
Light Olive Green   Dark Olive Green

Brooches - Petit Point Style

(Color photograph on inside back cover)

A contemporary petit point design can replace the traditional cameo or painted porcelain that would normally sit in an antique brooch frame.

You can design your own pattern or follow the two examples shown here. The antique frames were purchased in a store specializing in jewelry supplies. If you are unable to locate a brooch of the same size, the patterns can be adapted to most any other size. Simply extend or decrease the background areas to compensate for any difference in the dimensions.

MATERIALS:

No. 10/20 Penelope canvas, tapestry needle (no. 21 or no. 22), one-strand Persian yarn (suggested colors for brooch one: turquoise, yellow, off-white, green; suggested colors for brooch two: magenta, turquoise, white, gold, black), brooch frame, thin cardboard, felt for backing.

ALYSON S. GONSALVES

MODERN OR TRADITIONAL motif blends well with antique brooch frame. (Also see inside back cover.)

DIRECTIONS:

1. Cut and bind a piece of Penelope canvas 4 inches by 4 inches.
2. In the center of the canvas, outline the area to be needlepointed with an indelible marker (allow enough canvas for the tuck under). Brooch one covers an oval area approximately 1¼ inches by 1⅝ inches. Brooch two covers an oval area approximately 1⅝ inches by 1⅜ inches.
3. Separate the paired canvas threads within the oval outline making the canvas 20 stitches to the inch rather than 10.
4. Following the graph at right, stitch in all the detail and main designs, then fill in the larger background areas.
5. Once the stitching is completed, block the piece as explained on page 42. Machine stitch around the needlepointed section.
6. Trim the canvas edges to within ¼ inch of the stitching.
7. Cut a thin piece of cardboard the same dimensions and shape of the opening in the brooch. Spread a thin layer of white glue on the cardboard, then pull the edges of the needlepoint around it. Glue the canvas edges to the back, then glue another thin piece of cardboard over the back. After it has had some time to dry, push the piece into the brooch frame.
8. Cut two pieces of felt to cover the back of the brooch on either side of the clasp, then glue the two felt pieces into place.

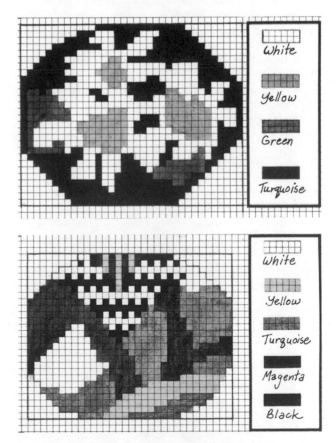

USE CHARTS or transfer pattern directly to canvas by reducing design 25%. Extend background for larger brooch.

One·Piece Casual Handbag

A needlepointed purse will be a durable and useful item you will carry with you for years. The example on the right is simple to assemble because it is made from one large needlepointed rectangle that is folded and lined. When purchasing the yarn for the project, choose colors complementary to your wardrobe.

MATERIALS:

No. 12 canvas, tapestry needle (no. 18 or no. 19), two or three-strand Persian wool (suggested colors: black, gray, cream, beige, brown), lining material, 9-inch plastic zipper.

DIRECTIONS:

1. Bind a piece of no. 12 canvas approximately 15 inches by 21 inches.
2. Using an indelible marker, outline border of the entire bag in the center of the canvas. Clearly indicate where the piece will fold (allow two to four meshes for the fold). This bag measures 11 inches wide by 17 inches long when unfolded or approximately 8½ inches deep when folded (101 meshes on each side).
3. Working the purse as one flat piece, stitch the complete design in basketweave and continental following the graph at right.
4. When stitching is completed, block the purse as explained on page 42.
5. Machine stitch around needlepointed section, then trim canvas edge to within 1 inch of stitching.
6. Turn under the edges but leave one unworked row of canvas beyond the two long sides of the needlepoint. Miter the corners as explained on page 45 and whip stitch the edges to the wrong side of the canvas.
7. Using the finished needlepoint as a pattern, cut a piece of closely woven lining cloth ⅝ inch larger on each side. Fold lining in half with right sides together; machine stitch the two sides together with a ⅝-inch seam. Put lining aside.

CATHARINE CRAFT

A NEEDLEPOINTED HANDBAG, like an oriental rug, becomes more beautiful with age and wear.

8. Fold needlepoint piece in half, matching the unworked mesh on the edges. Using the appropriate color yarn, join the sides by stitching a row of continental stitches or Gobelin stitches from the point of the fold to the top of the bag.
9. Push lining down into the needlepoint bag with wrong sides of needlepoint and lining facing each other. Turn top edge of lining under and stitch to inside top edge of needlepoint.
10. Using clear nylon thread, stitch top edges of purse together 1 inch in from each corner. Leave a 9-inch opening for the zipper.
11. Hand sew zipper into place (use instructions on zipper package).
12. With the remaining yarn, braid several strands into one long strap. Tie a knot at each end of the braid, then sew the knots to the corners of the bag.

Leave one unworked row
of canvas — sew together
using Gobelin or
Continental Stitch.

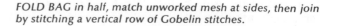

FOLD BAG in half, match unworked mesh at sides, then join by stitching a vertical row of Gobelin stitches.

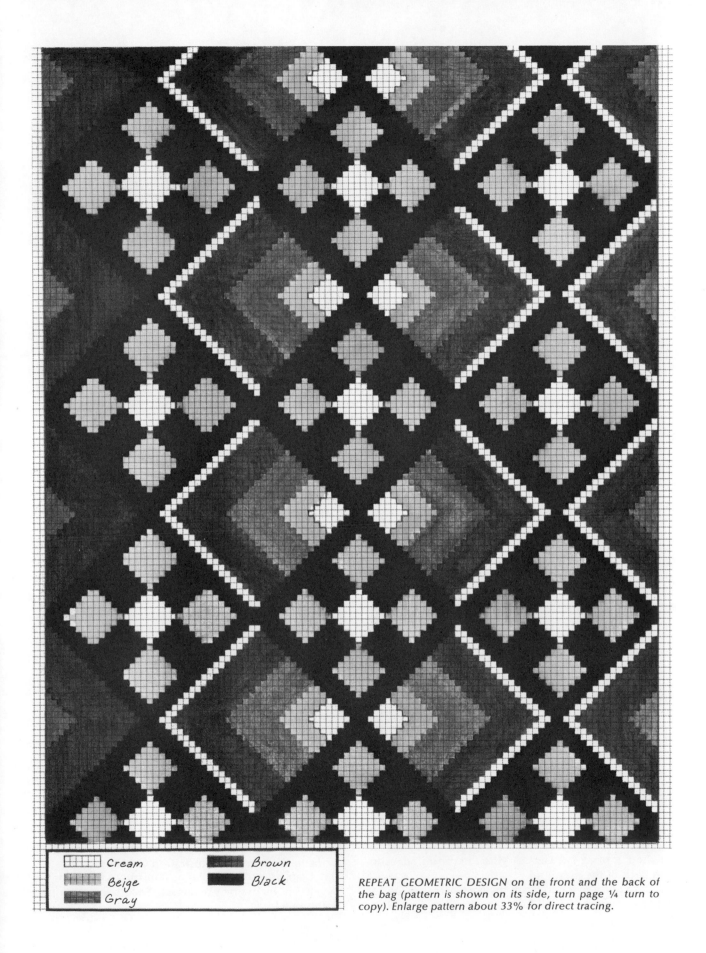

Cream
Beige
Gray
Brown
Black

REPEAT GEOMETRIC DESIGN on the front and the back of the bag (pattern is shown on its side, turn page ¼ turn to copy). Enlarge pattern about 33% for direct tracing.

Decorating the Hours

Hidden behind this attractive needlepointed face is the old forgotten electric or battery-operated clock. The needlepoint is simply a square mounted onto a thin masonite board, with the working parts of the clock attached to the back of the board. The entire clock face is stitched in continental and basketweave. You might consider using a decorative stitch (see pages 23-31) in either the large background area or central portion.

MATERIALS:

No. 10 mono canvas, tapestry needle (no. 18), three-strand Persian yarn (suggested colors: cocoa brown, beige, cream, white, navy blue, two shades of blue green), a small electric or battery-operated clock with removable arms (the battery clock is recommended), a square of masonite (9¾ inches), box-frame molding (allow enough for mitered corners).

DIRECTIONS:

1. Bind a piece of no. 10 mono canvas approximately 11¾ inches by 11¾ inches.
2. Using an indelible marker, outline the border of the clock face in the center of the canvas (suggested size: 9¾ inch square). Mark the center of each edge and the center of the design.
3. Trace enlarged design onto the canvas or follow the graph, opposite page. Since it is a geometric pattern, you may prefer following the graph and counting off stitches to be accurate.
4. Stitch the dark outlines and numbers first. Fill in center portion but leave a small unworked area in the exact center of the design (approximately two meshes by two meshes square). Stitch in the remaining areas.
5. After the stitching is completed, block the clock face as explained on page 42.
6. Cut a piece of masonite board just slightly smaller than the needlepoint (9¹¹⁄₁₆ inches). In the center of the board, drill a hole large enough for the movement mounting sleeve of the clock. Then mount the sleeve into position.
7. Machine stitch around the needlepointed section of the clock face and prepare the corners for mitering.
8. Trim the canvas edge to within 1 inch of the stitched section. Cut and miter corners of the needlepointed clock face around the masonite board (explained in method 2, page 45). Lace or glue the canvas edges to the back of the masonite.
9. Cut a piece of felt to cover the back of the masonite, cutting a hole in the felt for the mounting sleeve.

SUSAN S. LAMPTON

RUSSIAN IN ORIGIN, this geometric medallion pattern improves the appearance of a simple clock.

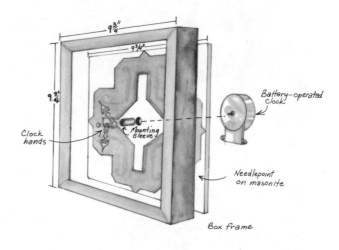

SECURE NEEDLEPOINT around masonite board. Slip board into frame and add clock and clock parts.

10. Mount the clock into position, then add the clock arms to the face (see illustration above).
11. Using box frame molding, construct a frame for the clock (9¾ inches by 9¾ inches). Secure the clock face into the frame.

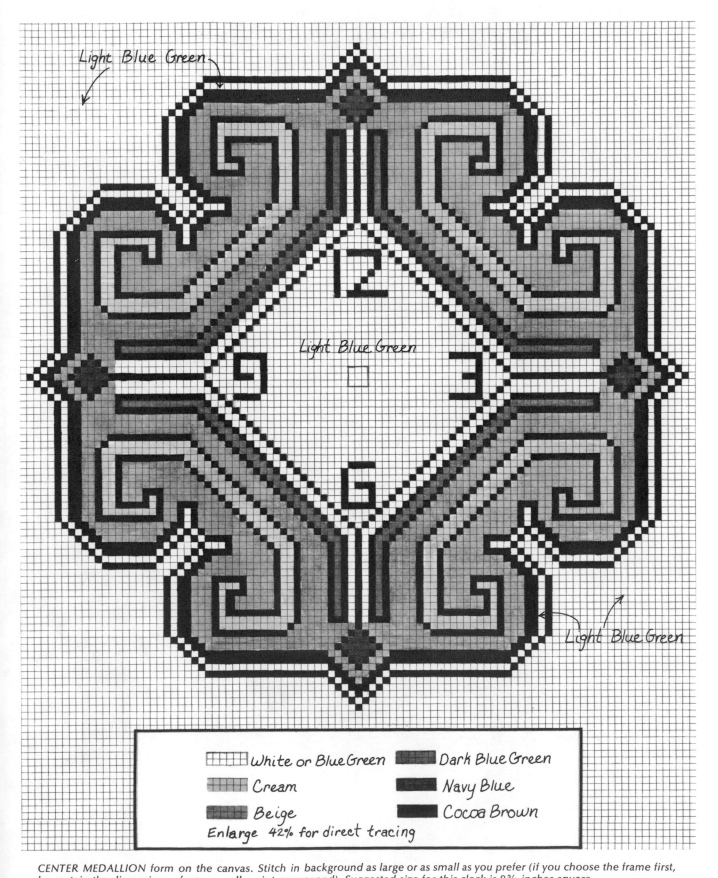

Light Blue Green

Light Blue Green

Light Blue Green

	White or Blue Green		Dark Blue Green
	Cream		Navy Blue
	Beige		Cocoa Brown

Enlarge 42% for direct tracing

CENTER MEDALLION form on the canvas. Stitch in background as large or as small as you prefer (if you choose the frame first, be certain the dimensions of your needlepoint correspond). Suggested size for this clock is 9¾ inches square.

Wild Animal Wastebasket

(Color photograph on inside front cover)

A wastebasket does not have to remain the unimaginative metal receptacle you once purchased. Give it a new look with a needlepoint covering and then display it in your living room or den. It may even become the perfect container for such things as dried flowers, rather than the storage bin for unwanted papers.

The tiger design on the wastebasket shown here has some detailed shading and modeling, but it is executed completely in the basketweave stitch. Penelope canvas is recommended because the teeth of the tiger are petit point.

MATERIALS:

No. 12 Penelope canvas, tapestry needle (no. 18 or no. 19), two-strand Persian yarn (suggested colors: rust, cocoa brown and purple twisted together, beige, light brown, cream, white, red, rose, chartreuse), a metal wastebasket with straight sides.

DIRECTIONS:

1. Measure the circumference of your wastebasket and add ½ inch to this measurement. Measure the height

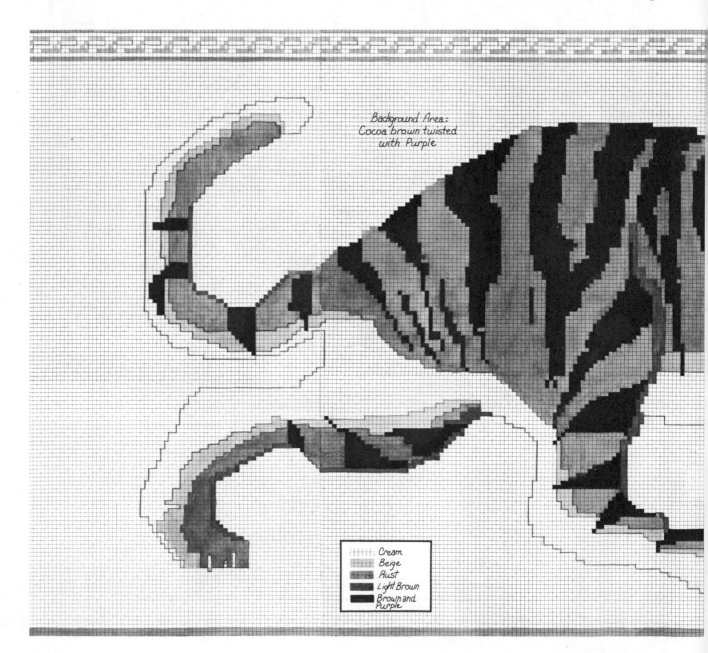

Background Area: Cocoa brown twisted with Purple

Cream
Beige
Rust
Light Brown
Brown and Purple

of the basket from just under the top rolled edge to the bottom rolled edge. This should give you the dimensions of the area to be needlepointed. Add 2 inches to each edge as a safety margin and for blocking purposes. Cut the measured canvas, then bind the edges.

2. Using an indelible marker, outline the border of area to be worked in the center of the canvas.

3. Trace the enlarged design onto the canvas or follow the graph shown below. Stitch entire tiger and border design in the basketweave stitch. Stitch the fangs of the tiger in petit point.

Continued on next page.

RENETTE C. SCOTT

TIGER AND BORDER should be stitched first. Enlarge design to size of the wastebasket for direct tracing.

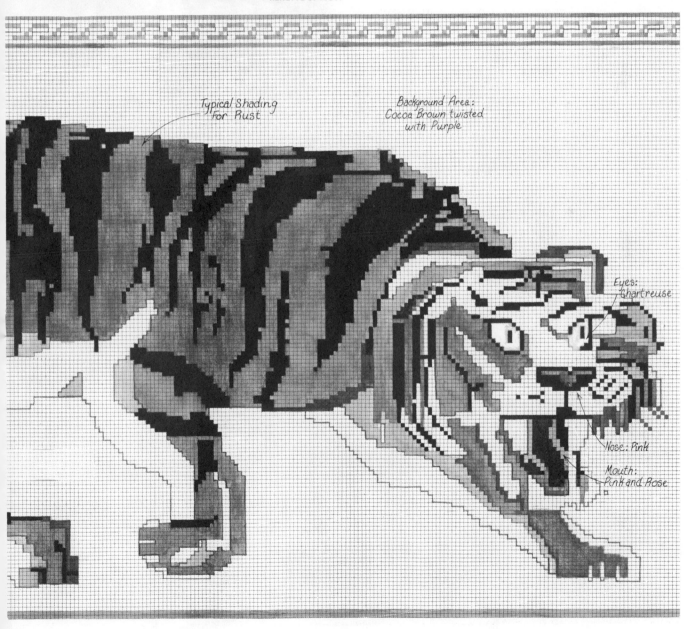

Typical Shading for Rust

Background Area: Cocoa Brown twisted with Purple

Eyes: Chartreuse

Nose: Pink

Mouth: Pink and Rose

Continued from previous page.

4. Stitch the background in basketweave, using one strand of brown and one strand of purple twisted together as one strand.

5. When completed, block the piece as explained on page 42.

6. Machine stitch around the needlepointed section. Trim the canvas edges to within 1 inch of the needlepoint. Turn under and whip stitch top and bottom canvas edges to wrong side of the needlepoint. Fold under the two ends that will be joined, leaving one unworked row of canvas beyond the needlepointed section. (See page 44.)

7. Fit the needlepoint around the basket, then, matching the mesh at the two ends, work one vertical row of continental stitches (see illustration at right). The covering should fit well but not so tightly that you can't remove it.

8. Carefully pull needlepoint off of the wastebasket. Spread a thin coat of clear drying glue over the entire surface of the wastebasket.

9. Slip the needlepoint back onto the basket and position the needlepoint directly under the rolled upper edge of the wastebasket. Immediately wipe off any glue that may have reached the needlepoint surface.

10. To prevent the needlepoint from slipping while the glue dries, tie two strings tightly around the top and bottom of the piece. Remove the string when the glue has completely dried.

SECURE NEEDLEPOINT on wastebasket by matching mesh along two ends, then stitch vertical row of stitches.

NEEDLEPOINT ALPHABETS

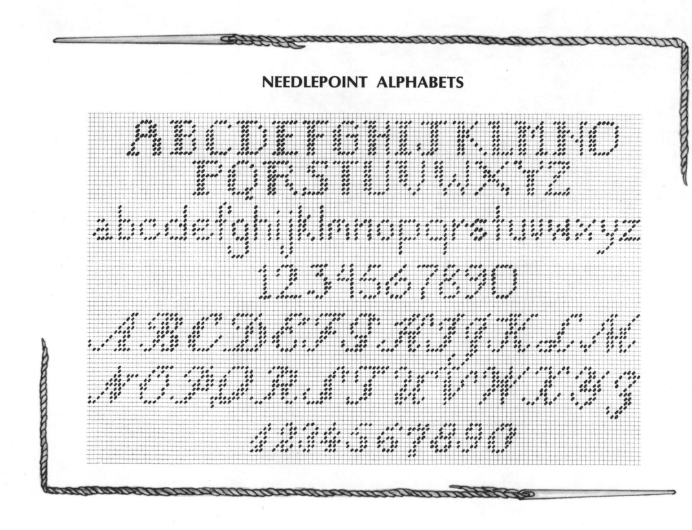

A Potpourri of Project Ideas

As you attempt more and more needlepoint projects, your search for transferable designs seems insatiable. Suddenly any object that has line, form, and color becomes a possibility for your needlepoint canvas. One good method of gathering new techniques and design ideas is to look at the accomplishments of other needleworkers. On the following four pages, several photographs are presented to inspire your artistic conceptions. These projects were created by professional as well as beginning needleworkers. Think of the most outrageous project you could do in needlepoint. Don't hold back, for, as you will discover, artists have attempted such monumental works as the 6 foot screen shown on page 78. You might consider upholstering your entire dining-room set of chairs.

Why not become the first person to ever needlepoint what seems to be impossible? Make your needlework an extension of your wildest dreams. Nothing is unchallengeable. Now that you have developed your ability and confidence, forge ahead with vigor!

ALICE MC CALLUM

MARY ALICE WILSON

ALYSON S. GONSALVES

DEDICATED TO THE SOON EXTINCT animal species, the vest (above) immortalizes such animals as the lion, zebra, and giraffe. Each of the animals is lovingly worked in petit point, but the background is worked in the simple and effective upright Gobelin stitch. The vest is completely handmade with a leather backing and satin lining. The queen of spades (above right) is detail of entire needlepointed card table cover. Four petit point cards mark the player's seat at the table. African design pillow (right) illustrates how an irregular line and bright colors can raise needlepoint to a level of sophisticated informality. (Also see inside front cover for color view.)

EACH PANEL of this 6 foot screen is dedicated to one of the children in the family of the artist. One panel took a year of devoted stitching. Monumental works such as this will be an heirloom for the family and a meaningful work of art.

MEMENTO OF THE famous San Francisco cable cars, this brick is cleverly transformed into a decorative door stop. Figures of people are all worked in petit point. The casing is constructed like the example on page 66, but extra blocks of wood were added at the top and the bottom.

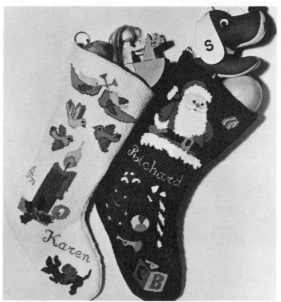

A FAMILY TREASURE to be displayed every Christmas is your traditional stocking worked completely in the Scottish stitch with details executed in petit point. The images on the stockings can symbolize the personality and interests of the owner.

MRS. JAMES M. R. GLASER

GINNY CAMPBELL AND MAZALTOV'S, INC.

RUGS worked in needlepoint will withstand many years of foot traffic. The elegant design of field mice and their natural predator, the owl, is a perfect design idea for any nature loving artist. This rug is about 4 feet square, an ambitious project for any needleworker to undertake. When making a rug, use sturdy canvas and good wool yarn.

BIRDS AND ANIMALS are always a natural subject for needlepoint. Both pillows shown above were worked on a very fine mesh canvas. The same method as explained on page 46 was used to make these box edged pillows. (Only the face of the pillow is needlepointed.) A Scottish stitch border frames the face of the tiger.

MRS. ROBERT SHOTWELL

KATHRYN SMITH CLINTON

GEOMETRIC PATTERNED BELT (above) simulates Indian bead work. The cross stitch is what creates this textural, beaded effect. The belt was lined then large snaps were added under the point of the belt as fasteners. (See page 57 for another belt design.) The pillow design (right) has a simple daisy form repeated in different sizes. To vary the texture, the center of each flower was worked in the French knot. The leaves were worked in the upright Gobelin stitch. Flowers are always an excellent design source but keep them simple and undetailed. Like this pillow, you can use texture as the major feature of a design. See pages 36-47 for techniques of making a pillow.

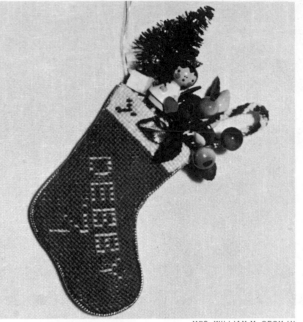

PERFECT FOR A CHILD'S ROOM, this friendly faced lion **(left)** is stitched with many different decorative stitches. The lion's mane is made from a stitch called turkey tufting. Other parts of his face have the mosaic stitch, diagonal mosaic stitch, Gobelin stitch, and, of course, basketweave. Even if you are an impatient needleworker, petit point can be enjoyable when it is worked on small items such as a Christmas tree decoration **(above)**. Stitch just the face of the stocking using a simple design. Back with velveteen then fill stocking with miniature gifts.

A RARE BIRD INDEED, this abstracted rooster is a simple but elegant design for a pillow. Several decorative stitches were combined to accentuate textural contrasts. The mosaic stitch seems particularly well suited for this angular design and the use of plain basketweave in the background makes the rooster rightfully the most prominent feature.

A DELFT TILE inspired the simple grasshopper design on the pillow above. As delicate as the design, the pillow is only about 8 inches square. Tile patterns are often a good design source because the images are usually greatly simplified. Why not make a coffee table topped with lovely picture tiles, then stitch a series of matching pillows for the couch?